KT-526-253

Credits

Authors

Purusothaman Ramanujam

Giorgio Natili

Reviewers

Ahmad Alrousan

Rafael Reyna Camones

Bhargav Golla

Steve Husting

Johnathan Iannotti

Razi Mahmood

Evan Mullins

Commissioning Editor

Usha Iyer

Acquisition Editor

Nikhil Karkal

Content Development Editor

Parita Khedekar

Technical Editor

Taabish Khan

Copy Editors

Trishya Hajare

Adithi Shetty

Project Coordinator

Suzanne Coutinho

Proofreader

Safis Editing

Indexer

Hemangini Bari

Production Coordinator

Nitesh Thakur

Cover Work

Nitesh Thakur

Foreword

The number of mobile devices and their usage is exploding rapidly across a wide variety of users around the world, heralding a series of very unique opportunities. For businesses, the opportunity to conceptualize new business applications and ideas, prototype, develop, and deliver these new capabilities to the market is very important. Customers benefit by being able to interact with brands and functions that have a direct and materially positive impact on their daily lives.

It sounds easy, but the major challenge today for a business is how to best support a dizzying array of mobile devices that are constantly evolving. Instead of targeting individual devices, such as the iPhone 6 or Samsung Galaxy 4, businesses begin to target device platforms, such as iOS, Android, and Windows Phone. Still, significant challenges remain when trying to quickly deliver powerful mobile application functionalities across multiple platforms.

This is where PhoneGap has such a significant role to play. Put simply, PhoneGap helps businesses develop mobile applications faster for a large variety of devices with minimum cost and time. To be successful, it's incredibly important to analyze the user's requirements upfront and then select the best tool and platform for development. Leveraging the correct APIs and programming models, techniques, and UX patterns can make the difference between a mobile application that is compelling and one that is too hard to use.

Keeping all of this in mind, this book seeks to educate developers on how to develop code in PhoneGap. As written by Purusothaman, I think you will find that this book is quite different from traditional development books. For example, each chapter is appropriately narrated for both the beginner and advanced level users. The examples covered in each chapter are simple and easy to understand but are still thorough enough to deliver important insights and lessons. The examples provided, and especially the sample project at the end, are very useful to PhoneGap programmers.

I would strongly recommend this book to those who want to get started with mobile application development or those who are already developing mobile applications to learn PhoneGap as a cross-platform tool to deliver compelling mobile applications.

Ranga Srinivasan
CTO & President, Ameex Technologies

About the Authors

Purusothaman Ramanujam is a mainframe consultant and an automation expert by profession and a full stack web developer and trainer by passion. He holds a bachelor's degree in information technology and a master's degree in financial management. He has a strong domain knowledge of financial markets. Apart from working full-time at a multinational corporation, he freelances and contributes to various open source projects. In his personal blog at `http://www.purusothaman.me`, he writes about technology, Tamil poetry, French, and more.

Giorgio Natili is an author, educator, community leader, and lead UI engineer at McGraw Hill Education; he is also a publisher of print and digital information services for the academic, professional, and library markets.

At McGraw Hill, he is involved with multiple client-side teams on cross-platform mobile and web applications, developing custom components (web and native) and bringing mock-ups to life!

Giorgio was also the founder of GNStudio, a boutique Rome-based development and design studio specializing in engaging and accessible web and mobile experiences.

As a strong proponent of agile development practices, Giorgio's areas of expertise include web standards-based application development, frontend development, gaming, video streaming, iOS development using Swift and Objective-C, Android development, and hybrid development (mobile and wearables).

Giorgio is the founder of Mobile Tea (`http://www.meetup.com/mobiletea/`), a fresh and innovative approach to community tech events, and is involved in several other community-driven events in Italy and the US.

About the Reviewers

Ahmad Alrousan has been a professional developer for many years, specializing in building desktop, web, and mobile software solutions for many sectors.

He holds a bachelor's degree in computer engineering and is a .NET Microsoft Certified Professional Developer (MCPD) and Microsoft Certified Solutions Developer (MCSD).

He spends a lot of time working on software projects and learning new skills. He can be reached at `alrosan@windowslive.com` (e-mail) and `http://sa.linkedin.com/pub/ahmad-alrousan/38/758/a8b` (LinkedIn).

He has also reviewed *Mobile First Design with HTML5 and CSS3, Jason Gonzales, Packt Publishing*, which was published in September 2013.

> I would like to thank my family, especially mom, for the continuous support they have given me throughout my life. I could not have done it without them.

Rafael Reyna Camones is an information technology consultant. He currently works at IBM as a software developer.

He has experience in the development of modules for Moodle and focuses on the integration of e-learning platforms with mobile devices (iOS, Android, and Windows Phone).

He graduated as a systems engineer from the Universidad Nacional José Faustino Sánchez Carrión. He has trained the university staff in the use of Moodle and has developed a pilot for implementation.

In his spare time, he enjoys a good conversation and exchange of ideas.

Other books reviewed by Rafael are *Instant Moodle Quiz Module How-to, Joan Coy*, and *Best Practices in Moodle Course Design, Susan Smith Nash and Michelle Moore*, both published by Packt Publishing.

Bhargav Golla is a master's student in computer science at Clemson University. Before going to Clemson, he graduated from Birla Institute of Technology and Science, Pilani, Pilani campus, with a B.E (Hons.) in computer science and engineering. Being chosen for the Google Summer of Code twice in a row, he had the pleasure of working with the open source organization Apache Software Foundation's projects Isis and PhotArk, where he built cross-platform mobile apps for the two projects. He believes in providing technical solutions to the problems we face. Interning at different tech companies in the past, he is currently looking forward to start his career as a developer.

Steve Husting wears various hats by day, including that of a website worker and product photographer, at a company that designs and manufactures radio-controlled hobby cars. By night, he writes, does calligraphy, and creates iPhone and Android apps. He posts his findings about PhoneGap apps on his blog, `http://iphonedevlog.wordpress.com`, which is geared up to help beginners get up and running in making cool apps. He also helped provide feedback for *PhoneGap 3.x Mobile Application Development Hotshot, Kerri Shotts, Packt Publishing*.

Johnathan Iannotti is a software engineer and geek on an epic journey of life. His experience spans 15 years of technology solutions for start-ups, financial companies, healthcare, and military industries. He is passionate about web technology and has been creating hybrid apps since their inception. A full-stack developer by trade, he loves UX/UI, frontend development, and mobile.

He works for USAA, creating mobile applications for over 27,000 employees who serve their military membership. He is also a combat veteran, having served almost a decade in the United States Army.

Johnathan spends his time innovating, coding, and making the best of it all. When he's not plugged in, he spends as much time as he can with his beautiful wife and two children, who make it all possible <3.

Follow Johnathan on Twitter at `@notticode` or visit his website at `www.johnforhire.com`.

Razi Mahmood is a software training consultant, currently active in delivering mobile apps development training in Malaysia. He covers Android, iOS, and PhoneGap/Cordova topics. His clients include Malaysian Development Corporation (MDEC), Malaysian Administrative Modernisation and Management Planning Unit (MAMPU), Ministry of Science, Technology and Innovation (MOSTI), Ministry of Finance, Ministry of Defense (MINDEF), Putrajaya Holdings Sdn Bhd, Kuala Lumpur City Hall, Petaling Jaya Municipal Council, Kota Bharu Municipal Council, Taiping Municipal Council, Penang Computer Center KOMTAR, and Kulim High Technology Park. He blogs at `www.razi.net.my`.

Evan Mullins studied digital media and earned his BFA at the University of Georgia, always interested in both design and technology. While attending, he also studied computer science, animation, and new media. He loves the cross-section of art and technology in which we find the Web.

Professionally, Evan has worked with a slew of start-ups, small businesses, and agencies, building websites such as Cartoon Network, Ogilvy & Mather, Brand Fever, and he is currently the lead web developer at Brown Bag Marketing. He is continually busy designing and developing interesting things online.

Since 2004, Evan has also maintained circlecube studio (`https://circlecube.com/`) as a freelance web studio and also a playground for open source experiments and examples, as well as to simply share tips he learns along the way. The blog content centers around interactive development principles and technologies. He gives back by sharing what he learns online as well as at conferences.

Evan is happily married and a proud father of four. He enjoys spending time away from work with his real job, his family. He also volunteers for his church and unplugs by camping outside, playing soccer, and/or playing music.

www.PacktPub.com

Support files, eBooks, discount offers, and more

For support files and downloads related to your book, please visit www.PacktPub.com.

Did you know that Packt offers eBook versions of every book published, with PDF and ePub files available? You can upgrade to the eBook version at www.PacktPub.com and as a print book customer, you are entitled to a discount on the eBook copy. Get in touch with us at service@packtpub.com for more details.

At www.PacktPub.com, you can also read a collection of free technical articles, sign up for a range of free newsletters and receive exclusive discounts and offers on Packt books and eBooks.

https://www2.packtpub.com/books/subscription/packtlib

Do you need instant solutions to your IT questions? PacktLib is Packt's online digital book library. Here, you can search, access, and read Packt's entire library of books.

Why subscribe?

- ◆ Fully searchable across every book published by Packt
- ◆ Copy and paste, print, and bookmark content
- ◆ On demand and accessible via a web browser

Free access for Packt account holders

If you have an account with Packt at www.PacktPub.com, you can use this to access PacktLib today and view 9 entirely free books. Simply use your login credentials for immediate access.

Always in memory of Rajeshwari Ramanujam

Ma,

I miss you every day...

Wish you were here to walk with me...

Smile as I talk about my first love...

Ask me about my day at work...

Wish you were here with us for everything...

I keep wondering every moment...

What you would think and feel about me...

I miss you Ma...

Table of Contents

Preface

PhoneGap Beginner's Guide Third Edition will help you break into the world of mobile application development. You will learn how to set up and configure your mobile development environment, implement the most common features of modern mobile apps, and build rich, native-style experiences. All the examples deal with real use case scenarios covering the functionality of various plugins.

What this book covers

Chapter 1, Introduction to PhoneGap, covers how to set up dependencies and mobile platform SDKs in your development environment.

Chapter 2, Building Your First PhoneGap Project, deals with PhoneGap internals, project structure, and using CLI tools.

Chapter 3, Mobile Frameworks, gives an introduction to various mobile frameworks and sample projects using jQuery Mobile.

Chapter 4, Working with Plugins, covers information about PhoneGap plugins and using them in the application.

Chapter 5, Using Device Storage and the Files API, deals with offline data storage capabilities and the Files plugin.

Chapter 6, Using the Contacts and Camera APIs, covers how to implement the Contacts API and how to interact with the device camera by using the Camera API.

Chapter 7, Accessing the Device Sensors and Locations API, deals with using device sensors and the Locations API and their power and limitations with respect to the plugins provided by PhoneGap.

Chapter 8, Advanced PhoneGap, covers some advanced topics such as adding multilanguage and touch gesture support to your application.

Chapter 9, Getting Ready for Release, helps you understand how to make your application ready for public release in various application stores.

Chapter 10, A Sample PhoneGap Project, deals with the development of a full-fledged PhoneGap application from scratch, using the most common PhoneGap plugins.

Appendix A, The JavaScript Quick Cheat Sheet, is a mini cheat sheet for commonly used JavaScript methods and properties.

Appendix B, Publishing Your App, describes how you can publish your apps on different app stores.

Appendix C, Related Plugin Resources, is a list of some related plugins that can be used with PhoneGap.

Appendix D, PhoneGap Tools, describes tools that will help you to debug and test your applications without any difficulties.

What you need for this book

A personal computer with an Internet connection and the default command-line tool to use with the command-line utilities distributed with PhoneGap. OS X and Linux users just need the default command-line tool.

Who this book is for

This book is for web developers who want to be productive in the mobile market quickly. In fact, by using PhoneGap, it's possible to deploy native applications based on web standards. This book assumes a very small knowledge of HTML/CSS/JavaScript and mobile platforms, such as Android, BlackBerry, iOS, and Windows Phone, and takes the reader step-by-step into a deep overview of PhoneGap and its APIs.

Sections

In this book, you will find several headings that appear frequently (Time for action, What just happened?, Pop quiz, and Have a go hero).

To give clear instructions on how to complete a procedure or task, we use these sections as follows:

Time for action – heading

1. Action 1
2. Action 2
3. Action 3

Instructions often need some extra explanation to ensure they make sense, so they are followed with these sections:

What just happened?

This section explains the working of the tasks or instructions that you have just completed.

You will also find some other learning aids in the book, for example:

Pop quiz – heading

These are short multiple-choice questions intended to help you test your own understanding.

Have a go hero – heading

These are practical challenges that give you ideas to experiment with what you have learned.

Conventions

You will also find a number of text styles that distinguish between different kinds of information. Here are some examples of these styles and an explanation of their meaning.

Code words in text, database table names, folder names, filenames, file extensions, pathnames, dummy URLs, user input, and Twitter handles are shown as follows: "You may notice that we used the Unix command `rm` to remove the `Drush` directory rather than the DOS `del` command."

A block of code is set as follows:

```
document.addEventListener("deviceready", function() {
    // Application starts here
});
```

When we wish to draw your attention to a particular part of a code block, the relevant lines or items are set in bold:

```
reader.onload = function(evt){

    var img = document.querySelector('#firstImage');
    img.src = evt.target.result;

};
```

Any command-line input or output is written as follows:

```
C:\example1> phonegap prepare android
```

New terms and **important words** are shown in bold. Words that you see on the screen, in menus or dialog boxes for example, appear in the text like this: "See the results in the console by clicking on the **Run** button at the bottom right of the panel."

 Warnings or important notes appear in a box like this.

Tips and tricks appear like this.

Reader feedback

Feedback from our readers is always welcome. Let us know what you think about this book— what you liked or disliked. Reader feedback is important for us as it helps us develop titles that you will really get the most out of.

To send us general feedback, simply e-mail feedback@packtpub.com, and mention the book's title in the subject of your message.

If there is a topic that you have expertise in and you are interested in either writing or contributing to a book, see our author guide at www.packtpub.com/authors.

Customer support

Now that you are the proud owner of a Packt book, we have a number of things to help you to get the most from your purchase.

Errata

Although we have taken every care to ensure the accuracy of our content, mistakes do happen. If you find a mistake in one of our books—maybe a mistake in the text or the code—we would be grateful if you could report this to us. By doing so, you can save other readers from frustration and help us improve subsequent versions of this book. If you find any errata, please report them by visiting http://www.packtpub.com/submit-errata, selecting your book, clicking on the **Errata Submission Form** link, and entering the details of your errata. Once your errata are verified, your submission will be accepted and the errata will be uploaded to our website or added to any list of existing errata under the Errata section of that title.

To view the previously submitted errata, go to https://www.packtpub.com/books/content/support and enter the name of the book in the search field. The required information will appear under the **Errata** section.

Piracy

Piracy of copyrighted material on the Internet is an ongoing problem across all media. At Packt, we take the protection of our copyright and licenses very seriously. If you come across any illegal copies of our works in any form on the Internet, please provide us with the location address or website name immediately so that we can pursue a remedy.

Please contact us at copyright@packtpub.com with a link to the suspected pirated material.

We appreciate your help in protecting our authors and our ability to bring you valuable content.

Questions

If you have a problem with any aspect of this book, you can contact us at questions@packtpub.com, and we will do our best to address the problem.

1

Introduction to PhoneGap

PhoneGap is a hybrid application framework that enables you to build native applications using HTML and JavaScript. Developers can write code once and deploy their application across multiple mobile operating systems. PhoneGap provides a JavaScript programming interface that allows you to access features related to the operating system with plain JavaScript. This chapter covers information about PhoneGap and setting up your development environment.

In this chapter, we will cover the following topics:

- ◆ Understanding what PhoneGap is all about
- ◆ Get an overview of the history of Apache Cordova/PhoneGap
- ◆ The evolution of PhoneGap and Cordova
- ◆ Learn the differences between the mobile web and mobile app
- ◆ Learn how to configure your development environment and all the dependencies
- ◆ Learn how to create a new project using JBoss, Xcode, and Visual Studio

About PhoneGap

PhoneGap, also called Apache Cordova, is an open source hybrid mobile application development framework. It uses standard and well-known web technologies such as HTML, **Cascading Style Sheets (CSS)**, and JavaScript to create cross-platform mobile applications without using native development languages.

If you want to develop a native Android application, you should know APIs related to Java and Android SDK. For an iPhone app, you need to know Objective-C or Apple's new Swift language. Similarly, for all other mobile platforms, you need to know their respective programming languages. The code you write for one platform does not work for another platform. To overcome these difficulties, we now have a hybrid mobile development framework called PhoneGap. The applications that you develop using PhoneGap can be deployed on several other platforms. It's a write-once-deploy-everywhere kind of framework.

The following is the list of mobile platforms currently supported by PhoneGap:

◆ Android
◆ iOS
◆ Amazon FireOS
◆ Blackberry 10
◆ Firefox OS
◆ Ubuntu
◆ Windows Phone 8
◆ Windows 8
◆ Tizen
◆ Windows 7
◆ Browser

The framework enables developers to access all the hardware-dependent features using simple JavaScript. Developers will be able to access device contacts, location, files, device information, and much more, with simple functions. Note that a new platform called "browser" is now supported. Sound interesting? It is left up to you to increase your curiosity.

PhoneGap and Apache Cordova

PhoneGap was originally developed by Nitobi and the company was later acquired by Adobe in 2011. After it was acquired, Adobe donated the PhoneGap code base to the **Apache Software Foundation (ASF)** under the project name **Cordova**, which is the name of the street in Vancouver where Nitobi's offices were located and where the company created the first version of PhoneGap.

One of the biggest advantages of moving the code base to the ASF is that anyone can easily contribute to the project. Many companies are not only comfortable with the Apache-flavored licenses but already have a Contributor License Agreement with Apache. For developers who are interested in contributing to a vibrant open source project, Apache Cordova is a great opportunity.

PhoneGap is a free and open licensed distribution of Apache Cordova. Picture Cordova as the engine on which PhoneGap and its related services (debug, emulate, and build services) are built. Adobe provides an integrated platform to build applications for multiple platforms with a single click. If you don't want to use Adobe's build features, you have to manually build applications for each mobile platform. Apart from these, for both PhoneGap and Cordova developers, nothing has changed.

Adobe continues to play a major role in the project, investing in its ongoing development, and the company decided to keep the PhoneGap name to describe its own distribution of the Cordova project. Other contributors to the Apache Cordova project include Google, RIM, Microsoft, IBM, Nokia, Intel, and Hewlett-Packard. For more details about Cordova and PhoneGap, refer to the following online resources. They have several useful bits of information and tutorials for a beginner to start with development:

 ◆ http://cordova.apache.org/
 ◆ http://phonegap.com/

 We will be using the terms PhoneGap and Cordova throughout this book and technically both are the same. You can replace Cordova and PhoneGap with each other.

The evolution of PhoneGap and Cordova

PhoneGap has evolved very quickly since January 2012, with multiple releases every year. Apache Cordova uses **Semantic Versioning** specification (more information is available at http://semver.org). It's a very good practice that tells developers whether a release has major or minor improvements.

Since the 1.4 release, the project has been known as Apache Cordova. This release is generally considered the first stable release of the framework, with a fairly complete and up-to-date documentation. The 1.5 release fixed a long list of bugs, but the initial reaction of the community was not very favorable because the documentation was outdated and some changes to the main files caused broken build issues to apps developed with earlier releases.

The 1.6 release brought some improvements to the plugin architecture, the Camera and Compass APIs, and the project template files. As is often the case with a maturing community, the release was not perfect but there was a significant improvement in the overall quality compared to the previous release. The 1.7 and 1.8 releases were bug fixes and added support for Bada 2.0. The community reaction was also positive because of the speed of the releases. The 1.9 release addressed even more bug fixes and added support for the new features of the iOS and Android platforms.

Apache Cordova 2.x added the following features and support:

♦ The definition of a unique JavaScript file to use across all platforms thanks to the unification of the JavaScript layer of the Cordova application framework

♦ The introduction of a command-line tool (CLI) through which common operations, such as project creation, debug, and emulation, could be performed in a standard way (Android, iOS, and BlackBerry)

♦ The capability to embed PhoneGap applications into larger native iOS and Android applications using Cordova WebView

♦ Support for the Windows phone platform

♦ The porting of the **Web Inspector Remote (Weinre)** to Node.js and the introduction of a node module that facilitates installation using **Node package manager** (**npm**)

♦ Improved plugin documentation

♦ Several improvements to the process of creating iOS apps

♦ The standardization of the commands available for each platform (that is, `build`, `run`, and so on)

With the 2.x release, Apache Cordova and PhoneGap has become a mature, stable, and powerful tool in the mobile developer's toolkit.

Since the introduction of version 3.0 in September 2013, PhoneGap has used a new plugin architecture to keep the application core small and fast performing. Plugins can be installed and uninstalled using the updated Cordova **command line interface** (**CLI**). PhoneGap 3.0 also introduced several new command-line tools; for instance, users can now install PhoneGap easily using npm without downloading ZIP files. Two new APIs, namely InAppBrowser (earlier known as ChildBrowser) and Globalization API were also released with the PhoneGap 3.0 release. They also started discussions about dropping support for webOS, Symbian, Blackberry (BB7 and earlier versions), and Windows Phone 7.

With PhoneGap 3.1.0, basic support for FirefoxOS and Windows 8 were provided along with other bug fixes and platform enhancements. PhoneGap 3.2.0, released in November 2013, was focused on stability and several bug fixes. In December 2013, PhoneGap 3.3.0 was released with support for Android KitKat (v4.4).

With the release of PhoneGap 3.4.0, advanced support for FirefoxOS was added. PhoneGap 3.5.0 is the last version supporting Windows 7. With PhoneGap 3.6.3, commands supported by Cordova were added. There are several new features deployed to PhoneGap with every new release. At the time of authoring this book, we have PhoneGap 5.1.1, which provides advanced support for the PhoneGap Desktop App and Mobile App.

Choosing an operating system for development

PhoneGap plays by the rules. If a vendor releases an SDK for a single operating system only, then you will have to use that OS to build and deploy your applications.

In detail, for each PhoneGap platform:

- You can develop **Android** apps on any of the major desktop operating systems— Windows, Mac OS X, or Linux
- You can develop **Symbian Web Runtime** apps on any OS but you can only run the simulator from Windows
- You can develop apps for **BlackBerry** on any of the major desktop operating systems—the SDK can be installed on Windows or Mac OS X (to run the emulator, you need to install the virtual machine distributed with the SDK)
- The **Windows Phone 8** SDK runs on Windows 8 or Windows 8 Pro
- The **iOS** SDK requires OS X 10.7 or later (and, according to the OS X EULA, a Mac computer as well)

> You can emulate apps in the desktop browser with Ripple (a Chrome extension that is currently incubated in the Apache Software Foundation http://incubator.apache.org/projects/ripple.html) or with the online emulation service available at http://emulate.phonegap.com.

Practically speaking, your best bet for mobile development is to get a Mac and install Windows on a separate partition that you can boot into, or run it in a virtual environment using **Parallels** or **VMWare Fusion**. According to Apple's legal terms, you cannot run Mac OS X on non-Apple hardware; if you stick with a Windows PC, you will be able to build for every platform except iOS. However, you can still use OS X by using VirtualBox and running OS X from a Windows PC.

Anyway, with the new CLI utilities, it is getting to be pretty easy to build an app for all major mobile platforms. Mobile developers are well aware of the problems involved in building cross-platform apps; not surprisingly, the `http://build.phonegap.com` service is starting to become pretty popular due to the fact that it lets the developer use his/her favorite operating system. After registering with this service, it's possible to build a cross-platform app starting from a common code base. You can upload the code base or pull it from a GitHub repository. At the end of this book, I have included a section dealing with the distribution process for mobile applications.

Mobile web versus mobile app

There are lots of discussions that are centered around deciding what kind of development should be done: mobile-responsive websites or a native app. Some popular websites, such as Gmail, have mobile-friendly websites, as well as native apps. To understand this better, let's see what these are:

Responsive websites	Mobile app
Responsive websites work across all kinds of devices, starting from mobile devices to desktop computers. This way of design is often called **Responsive Web Design (RWD)**.	Applications are designed for mobile devices. They are not meant for desktop computers.
Responsive designs provide a better viewing experience to the users on all devices.	A mobile application gives a typical mobile experience with the entire interface designed with mobile devices in mind.
RWD involves some development concepts such as fluid grid, CSS media queries, responsive tables, and images.	Mobile-related design patterns are used.
Responsive sites adapt well to the device's screen size, which makes reading the content easier.	Content is usually designed for mobile screen sizes. Readability is always better.
Mobile web is a normal website, which adapts to mobile devices.	Mobile apps have the power of doing more than a simple website.
Responsive design is a cost-effective alternative to mobile applications.	Dedicated development and time needs to be invested for application development.
As with any other website, they are restricted to the features of browser.	Provides rich user experience by using several device-related APIs such as Camera, Accelerometer, and so on.

For more information about RWD and the design principles behind it, please read the fundamentals at `https://developers.google.com/web/fundamentals/layouts/rwd-fundamentals/`.

To summarize, both RWD and mobile apps have advantages and disadvantages. It's the goal of your business or requirement that decides which one you are going to develop. If you are going to develop mobile applications, you should be targeting multiple mobile platforms and it's not quite possible to code for all platforms within a short time frame. Here comes the power of hybrid mobile applications developed using PhoneGap.

Installing dependencies

In order to be ready to build a PhoneGap app, it's mandatory to download and install the latest SDKs for each target platform of the app from the respective official websites:

- **Android**: `http://developer.android.com/sdk/index.html`
- **BlackBerry 10**: `https://developer.blackberry.com/html5/downloads/#blackberry10`
- **Firefox OS**: No special SDKs are required
- **iOS**: `https://developer.apple.com/devcenter/ios/index.action`
- **Windows 8 Phone**: `http://www.microsoft.com/en-in/download/details.aspx?id=35471`

Each of the preceding platform SDKs have their own setup configuration and it's advised to refer to the respective websites for updated information. To use several IDEs, such as NetBeans, Eclipse, or JBoss Developer Studio, we need Java to be available.

Java JDK

You need to install the most recent **Java JDK** (not just the JRE). Next, create an environment variable for `JAVA_HOME`, pointing to the root folder where the Java JDK was installed. For example, if your installation path is `C:\Program Files\Java\jdk7`, set `JAVA_HOME` to be this path. After that, add the JDK's `bin` directory (`C:\Program Files\Java\jdk7\bin`) to the `PATH` variable as well.

Apache Ant

We need **Apache Ant** to be installed and configured. Update your `PATH` to include the `bin` folder in the installation folder. For advanced configuration details, visit `http://ant.apache.org/manual/index.html`.

Due to the latest changes in the PhoneGap framework, it's always suggested to use the command-line interface to create a new project, update the framework, or install plugins. To work with the command line, we will need the **Node.js** application. To start with, download and install Node.js from `http://nodejs.org`. Once you have done this, you should be able to verify the installation by invoking `npm` or `node` on your command line. You may need to add the `npm` directory to your system `PATH` in order to invoke globally-installed npm modules.

At the end of every installation, you should be able to verify the installations of each package with the following commands:

```
android list sdk
javac -version
ant -version
node -v
```

If any of the preceding command lines don't work as required, you might need to revisit your system `PATH` settings. For example, PhoneGap and Cordova require the `ANDROID_HOME` environment variable to be set in `PATH`. This should point to the `[ANDROID_SDK_DIR]\android-sdk` directory (for example, `c:\android\android-sdk`).

Next, update your `PATH` to include the `tools/` and `platform-tools/` folders. So, using `ANDROID_HOME`, you would add both `%ANDROID_HOME%\tools` and `%ANDROID_HOME%\platform-tools`.

For OS X users, it is also important to install ios-sim. The ios-sim tool is a command-line utility that launches an iOS app on the simulator. To install the tool, you can again use npm, as shown here:

```
npm install -g ios-sim
```

Depending on your privileges, you may have to run the `npm` command as an administrator (that is, adding `sudo` before the `npm` command).

Once the SDKs are installed, it's recommended that you also install the client for GitHub. GitHub is a social coding platform where you can find most of the cool open source projects (such as Apache Cordova), including access to the latest patches, builds, and sources. You can easily build your project for multiple platforms using PhoneGap's free online build service from a public GitHub repository.

Installing PhoneGap

Starting from Apache Cordova 2.0, the installation process and the setting up of your development environment has become much easier. Before the era of 2.0, the installation process of PhoneGap had been confusing because there were a lot of dependencies. These dependencies were due to the fact that, in order to compile an app for different platforms, you not only had to have the platform-specific SDKs but also the platform-specific tools; for example, in order to build for Android, Eclipse, IntelliJ, or Android Studio were required; to build for iOS, Xcode was required; and so on.

You can now use a set of command-line tools shipped with Cordova, which makes it easier to develop cross-platform applications. Installing Cordova and PhoneGap is now as easy as issuing a few commands. Please note that we can use CLI commands related to Cordova or PhoneGap. The PhoneGap CLI offers more added features than its Cordova counterpart such as support for PhoneGap Desktop and Mobile app.

To kick-start the development, let's create a new project. We will use the npm utility Node.js to automatically download the latest framework code.

In the Windows environment, issue the following command:

```
C:\>npm install -g phonegap
```

On Linux and OS X, issue the following command:

```
$ sudo npm install -g phonegap
```

By using the -g flag in the preceding command, we instruct npm to install PhoneGap globally; otherwise, it will be installed in the current directory. Once the installation process is done, verify the installation by issuing the following command in the command-line terminal. This should return the latest version number of PhoneGap.

```
phonegap --version
```

Once we have verified the Cordova installation, we can create a new app project by using the following command:

```
phonegap create hello
```

It may take some time for this command to complete. This is the minimal syntax required to create a project where `hello` is the project name. A new folder named `hello` will be created in the current working directory. The directory content will be as shown here:

```
├── hooks
├── merges
├── platforms
├── plugins
├── www
│   └── css
│   └── img
│   └── js
│   └── index.html
├── config.xml
```

In the www folder, you'll find the HTML/JS/CSS files needed to run the sample PhoneGap app bundled with the binary of the distribution.

Setting up your development environment

This section provides a detailed guide to setting up the Android, iOS, and Windows Phone development environments. In order to set up a development environment based on a simple text editor, it suffices to run a few commands using the command-line tool.

Time for action – setting up Android using PhoneGap 3.x

Get ready to set up the Android development environment and create a PhoneGap app using Android as the target platform. In the previous section, we saw how to create a new project. Now it's time to add the desired platform to the project. As usual, use Terminal on OS X or DOS Prompt on Windows to run these commands.

1. Launch a command-line tool (DOS or Terminal) and change the directory to the directory where we just downloaded the Cordova/PhoneGap distribution, as shown here:

    ```
    $ cd hello
    ```

2. In order to create a PhoneGap project for Android, all you have to do is run the command to add a platform to the project:

    ```
    $ phonegap platform add android
    ```

The command tells Cordova to add support for the Android platform. After the successful execution of the command, you can see a new directory named `android` created inside the platform directory. This contains all the platform-dependent files.

Now it's time to run the project in the emulator. The following command will take some time to complete:

```
$ phonegap emulate android
```

The tool will check whether some virtual devices are already defined and prompt the user to define one if not. If there is more than one device already defined, the tool will ask which one to use.

What just happened?

You created a PhoneGap project and emulated the app in one of the testing devices configured within your Android SDK.

Working with other platforms

To work with different platforms such as iOS, Windows Phone, and others, you have to follow the same process that we did for Android. The list of platforms that you can add to your project depends on the platform name. Before you add the platforms, you should ensure that you have the required SDKs installed on your machine.

On a Windows machine, you can run any of the following commands provided you have the required SDKs installed for each platform. You will not see the iOS platform here as we need a Mac machine to work on iOS:

```
C:\hello> phonegap platform add wp7
C:\hello> phonegap platform add wp8
C:\hello> phonegap platform add windows8
C:\hello> phonegap platform add amazon-fireos
C:\hello> phonegap platform add android
C:\hello> phonegap platform add blackberry10
C:\hello> phonegap platform add firefoxos
```

In the preceding commands, `wp7` and `wp8` denote Windows Phone 7 and 8, respectively.

On a Mac machine, you can develop on the following platforms after installing the corresponding platform SDKs. You will not see the Windows Phone platform here as we need the Windows operating system to install the Windows Phone SDK:

```
$ phonegap platform add ios
$ phonegap platform add amazon-fireos
$ phonegap platform add android
$ phonegap platform add blackberry10
$ phonegap platform add firefoxos
```

Getting started with Android and JBoss

There are several IDEs for Java and a few of them are **IntelliJ IDEA**, **Eclipse**, **NetBeans**, and **JBoss Developer Studio**. Android Studio is the most recommended and commonly used IDE for Android development. However, it does not provide support for Cordova/PhoneGap development. When compared to others, JBoss Developer Studio provides a very easy and convenient way of creating and working with the PhoneGap project. You can download the latest version from the JBoss website at `https://www.jboss.org/products/devstudio/download/`. In order to run a sample application based on Apache Cordova/PhoneGap, you need to install the Android SDK, and add the **JBoss Hybrid Mobile Tools** plugin to your JBoss install. This tool extends the capabilities of JBoss to let you quickly set up new Cordova projects, add Cordova plugins, debug applications, and even export signed (or unsigned) APK files in order to distribute the application.

Time for action – using JBoss Developer Studio

In order to install Hybrid Mobile Tools into JBoss, it's enough to perform the following steps:

1. Start JBoss Developer Studio and then navigate to **Help | JBoss Central**.
2. Click on the **Software/Update** tab in JBoss Developer Central.
3. Type `JBoss Hybrid Mobile Tools` or scroll through the list to locate **JBoss Hybrid Mobile Tools + CordovaSim**.
4. Select the corresponding checkbox and click on **Install**.
5. When prompted to restart the IDE after installation, click on **Yes** to restart JBoss Developer Studio.

Once the JBoss Hybrid Mobile Tools installation is properly configured, it's possible to create a new project using the appropriate wizard.

Go to **JBoss Hybrid Mobile Tools | New | Other**. Next, select **Hybrid Mobile (Cordova) Application Project** in the **Mobile** section. Click on **Next**:

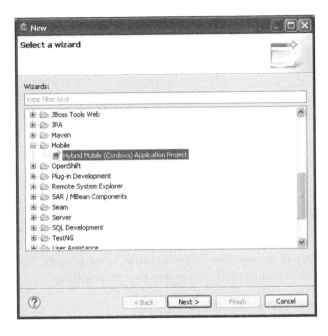

Enter the values for **Project name**, **Name**, and **ID**. We will use example for **Name** and org.example for **ID**, as shown in the following screenshot:

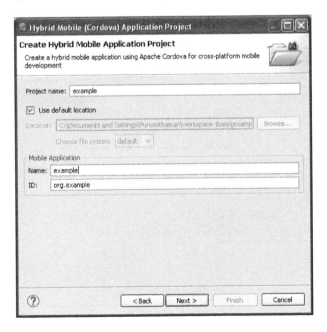

Click on **Next** to see the options to select which Cordova version to use. Let's always go with the latest version:

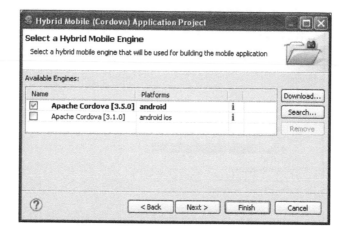

Clicking on **Next** again will present the option to install some plugins. For this tutorial, we don't need any plugins to be installed. So we don't select anything.

Click on **Finish** to exit the wizard.

At the end of the wizard, a default application will be created for you. Now let's build the created application and see how it looks on the emulator. Click on the **Run As** toolbar icon and select the **Run with CordovaSim** option to open the simulator:

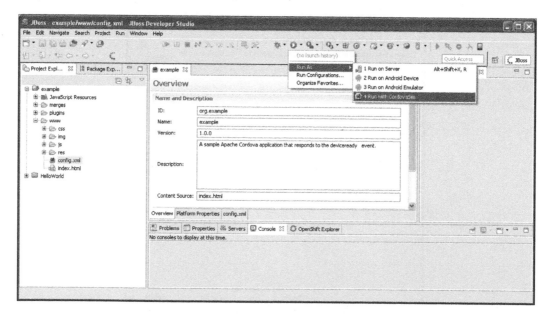

What just happened?

Once the build process is done, you will see an emulator on the screen. With this, we are now able to create a new project and emulate it successfully:

Getting started with iOS and Xcode

In order to start developing apps for iOS devices, it's mandatory to have a Mac and download the iOS SDK (Xcode), available on the Apple Developer Center at `http://developer.apple.com`. Complete the following steps to install Xcode:

1. Install Xcode from the App Store.
2. Install the Xcode command-line tools (**Xcode Preferences | Downloads | Components | Command Line Tools | Install**).

Now, let's create an iOS project using the command-line tools, as shown here:

```
$ phonegap create hello
$ cd hello
$ phonegap platform add ios
$ phonegap build
```

Once the preceding commands are executed, you will have the Xcode project created. You can see the `hello/platforms/ios/hello.xcodeproj` file and you can double-click on it to open it. With this, our project is already set up and ready to be debugged and deployed.

In order to deploy the app, change **Target** in the **Scheme** drop-down menu on the toolbar to **Hello** (or the current project name) and change **Active SDK** in the **Scheme** drop-down menu on the toolbar to **iOS [version] Simulator**. Once you have done this, click on the **Run** button.

> If you are searching for a tool for Objective-C with advanced refactoring features, better code completion, great support for unit tests, and powerful code inspection tools, you should consider buying **AppCode** from **JetBrains**. More information is available at `http://www.jetbrains.com/objc/`.

Getting started with Windows Phone and Visual Studio

Microsoft Visual Studio now has plugins for multi-device hybrid apps, including Cordova, which allows you to run and debug apps on an Android/Windows Phone. If you want to debug the app on a real device, you have to create a developer account at `https://dev.windowsphone.com/en-us/account` in order to unlock the option to debug a real device.

Summary

In this chapter, you learned how to set up your development environment using the CLI tools included in Apache Cordova and working with several platforms. The next chapter will help you choose a development environment and show you how to debug your first app on multiple platforms.

2
Building Your First PhoneGap Project

In Chapter 1, Introduction to PhoneGap, you learned about one of the problems PhoneGap is trying to solve—developing mobile applications consistently across multiple platforms—and how to set up your build environment. Next, you will delve into the internals of PhoneGap. First, you need to know how the project is structured and how the CLI tools are used.

In this chapter, you will:

- ◆ Take a look at the structure of a PhoneGap/Cordova application
- ◆ Learn about using the command-line tools of Cordova
- ◆ Know about Cordova lifecycle events
- ◆ Create a sample example
- ◆ Get an overview of the browser's debugging tools
- ◆ Review the debug workflow with mobile in mind
- ◆ Learn how to build and deploy the applications

The structure of a PhoneGap application

After creating a new project, as explained in the previous chapter, you'll see the following structure inside the project's root folder:

- ◆ www: This directory contains the source files of the application and so we will be playing a lot in this directory. It contains the css, js, and img subdirectories, where you can place the respective files. Apart from assets such as CSS, JavaScript, and images, we will also have application-related HTML files.

- ◆ merges: In this folder, you can add any platform-specific customization so you don't have to modify the source files every time you work with a project. For example, we can use this feature to use a different font style on Android devices only. The platforms that you want to override will have a specific folder similar to the www folder having its own CSS, JS, HTML, and image contents:

```
merges/
|-- ios/
|    '-- app.js
|-- android/
|    '-- app.js
www/
'-- app.js
```

  In the preceding directory structure, the global application has the app.js file and in the merges directory, each platform has a separate app.js file. During the build process, the global app.js file will be replaced with the platform-specific app.js file.

- ◆ platforms: This directory will have platform-dependent build files. For each platform that we add to the project, we can see a subdirectory.

- ◆ plugins: This is the directory where you'll find the plugins used in the project. Whenever we install new plugins, they will be added over here.

- ◆ hooks: This directory can contain scripts that can be used to customize the Cordova/PhoneGap commands. This is really for advanced users where integrating with build systems and version control systems is required.

- ◆ config.xml: This configuration file will have all the values specific to the application, such as application name, package name, version number, and other such configurations.

Using the PhoneGap CLI

You can use the Cordova command-line interface to initialize the project code, after which you can use various platforms' SDKs to develop them further. In the previous chapter, we discussed how to create a new project, add the required platforms, and build them using the CLI.

Apart from creating a project by using the CLI tool, there are several other functions carried out by the CLI of Cordova. As the steps for installing the CLI are already covered, let's move on with advanced CLI usage. Once you create a project, use cd to move into it and you can execute a variety of project-level commands.

The following is the list of the most used CLI commands:

- `platform add <platform>`: This adds a platform as a build target for the project.
- `platform [rm | remove] <platform>`: This removes a platform which was previously added to the project.
- `platform [ls | list]`: This lists all platforms for which the project will build.
- `platform [up | update] <platform>`: This updates the Cordova version used for the given platform.
- `plugin [ls | list]`: This lists all the plugins included in the project.
- `plugin add <path-to-plugin> [<path-to-plugin> ...]`: This adds one (or more) plugins to the project.
- `plugin [rm | remove] <plugin-name> [<plugin-name> ...]`: This removes one (or more) plugins from the project.
- `plugin search [<keyword1> <keyword2> ...]`: This searches the plugin registry for plugins matching the list of keywords.
- `prepare [platform...]`: This copies files into the specified platforms, or all platforms. It is then ready for building by Eclipse, Xcode, and so on.
- `compile [platform...]`: This compiles the app into a binary for each targeted platform. With no parameters, it builds for all platforms; otherwise, it builds for the specified platforms.
- `build [<platform> [<platform> [...]]]`: This is an alias for cordova prepare followed by cordova compile.
- `emulate [<platform> [<platform> [...]]]`: This launches emulators and deploys the app to them. With no parameters, it emulates the app for all the platforms added to the project; otherwise, it emulates the app for the specified platforms.
- `serve [port]`: This launches a local web server allowing you to access each platform's www directory on the given port (default 8000).

All the preceding CLI commands are to be executed inside the project directory. Some of the example usages are as follows:

```
c:\hello>phonegap platform add android
c:\hello>phonegap platform add ios
c:\hello>phonegap platform remove android
c:\hello>phonegap platform list
```

The `help` command is a global command, which displays a help page with all the available commands and the syntax to use them. This command can be executed at any command window and not necessarily within the project directory:

```
c:\> phonegap help
```

Cordova events

To maximize the benefits of using Cordova, you should know about all the events available. They are called **lifecycle events** because they are a part of your application throughout its lifecycle. These events are available by default for all applications and it's up to the developer to use them to implement better design. Although there are several events, we will discuss the most important and commonly used events.

The deviceready event

The `deviceready` event is an important event of Cordova and you can't live without it in the Cordova world. This event is triggered when Cordova has fully loaded and the application is ready to be used. We should know when the application is ready to be used and so this event comes to our rescue. This event should be the gateway to all the application's functionality:

```
document.addEventListener("deviceready", function() {
    // Application starts here
});
```

To make the code easy to understand, we can define the function separately and bind it to the event, as shown here:

```
document.addEventListener("deviceready", onDeviceReady);

function onDeviceReady() {
        // Application starts here
}
```

The online event

The online event is triggered when the device goes online with Internet connectivity. With this event, you can determine whether your application is currently in the online state or not. If your application requires the user to be online, this can be helpful:

```
document.addEventListener("online", onOnline);

function onOnline() {
    console.log('device is now online');
}
```

The offline event

As you might have guessed, the offline event is the opposite of the online event. When the device goes offline, the application can capture it by using this event and necessary action can be taken by the developer:

```
document.addEventListener("offline", onOffline);

function onOffline() {
    console.log('device is now offline');
}
```

 There is no accurate way of finding whether the device is currently in the **online** or **offline** state. These events work on the connection state and it can sometimes be wrong. Note that even though the device is connected to 2G, 3G, or Wi-Fi, it doesn't mean the device is online.

The pause event

The pause event is triggered when the application is moved to the background, which is typically when the user switches to another application. You can use this event to notify users that they are being taken away from the application:

```
document.addEventListener("pause", onPause);
```

The resume event

When the application is again brought to the foreground, the resume event is triggered. This usually happens after the pause event as the app should be in the background before coming to the foreground of the mobile platform:

```
document.addEventListener("resume", onResume);
```

The backbutton event

The backbutton event is fired when the user presses the Back button on the mobile device. You can use this event to override the default actions that happen when the Back button is pressed:

```
document.addEventListener("backbutton", onBackbutton);
```

There are several other events that are supported by external plugins. There is an exhaustive list of such plugins, which can be used by adding the appropriate plugins to the project.

 Not all events are supported on all platforms. For example, the backbutton event is not supported on iOS devices. For the full list of supported platforms for each event, refer to the documentation at http://cordova.apache. org/docs/en/edge/cordova_events_events.md.html#Events.

Time for action – the Hello World example

PhoneGap is an intermediary layer that talks to the mobile device and the application; the app resides inside a browser, and, using the PhoneGap API, you can connect to phone features such as contacts and camera.

The UI layer of a PhoneGap application is a web browser view that takes up 100 percent of the device's width and height; think of the UI layer as a browser. The UI layer is known as **WebView**. The WebView used by PhoneGap is the same one used by the native operating system.

Having discussed the basics of PhoneGap and the command-line tools, we will now create a simple application. This is not the typical Hello World example. With the already learned commands and configured environment with npm, let's create a new project:

```
C:\> phonegap create example1
C:\> cd example1
C:\example> phonegap platform add android
```

With the completion of the preceding commands, we created a new project called
`example1` and added Android platform support to the project. The directory structure
is now this:

```
example1
├── config.xml
├── hooks
├── merges
├── platforms
├── plugins
    └── android
├── www
    └── css
    └── img
    └── js
    └── index.html
```

By default, the Cordova `create` script generates a skeletal web-based application whose
home page is the project's `www/index.html` file. Edit this application however you want,
but any initialization should be specified as part of the `deviceready` event handler,
referenced by default from `www/js/index.js`.

When you open the `index.html` file present in the `www` directory, you will see HTML code.
The `body` section will be similar to the code presented here. This is the default body content
generated by the CLI tool for the project. It just shows a page with an image and some text:

```html
<body>
    <div class="app">
        <h1>Apache Cordova</h1>
        <div id="deviceready" class="blink">
            <p class="event listening">Connecting to Device</p>
            <p class="event received">Device is Ready</p>
        </div>
    </div>
    <script type="text/javascript" src="cordova.js"></script>
    <script type="text/javascript" src="js/index.js"></script>
    <script type="text/javascript">
        app.initialize();
    </script>
</body>
```

The output would be the following:

For a complex application, the page would not be this simple. To start with, let's modify the page to add some text. The modified code is shown here, which is a simple static HTML content:

```html
<body>
    <h1>First Project</h1>
    <h3>What we have learnt?</h3>
    <ul>
      <li>PhoneGap Structure</li>
      <li>CLI Commands</li>
      <li>Developer Tools</li>
      <li>Debugging in Browsers</li>
      <li>Cordova Events</li>
    </ul>
    <script type="text/javascript" src="cordova.js"></script>
    <script type="text/javascript">
      document.addEventListener('deviceready', deviceready, false);
      function deviceready() {
        alert("Example Event");
      }
    </script>
</body>
```

If any JavaScript external files are included at the top of the HTML `head` section, the browser stops parsing further until the file is downloaded. So it is recommended to add any JavaScript files or code chunks to the end of the `body` tag to decrease the wait time.

Today, most modern browsers support the `async` and `defer` attributes on scripts. These attributes tell the browser that it's safe to continue parsing while the scripts are being downloaded:

```
<script type="text/javascript" src="path/to/script1.js"
  async></script>
<script type="text/javascript" src="path/to/script2.js"
  defer></script>
```

What just happened?

We removed the code from the default project created and added our own content. Please note that we added the `deviceready` event listener. When the app gets loaded and ready for action, the event will show an alert box. The `deviceready` event should be the entry point for all our device-related action.

When we build and emulate the sample project, we will see the following output in the emulator:

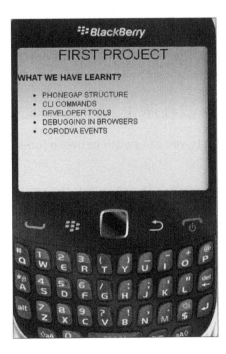

WebKit debugging – Chrome, Safari, and Opera

WebKit-based browsers support various debugging tools. For example, when encountering JavaScript issues, you can launch Web Inspector or Developer Tools and start to explore logs and errors using the JavaScript console.

In Chrome, you can access the Developer Tools from the Customize menu (click on the Customize menu and then go to **Tools | Developer Tools**). The Customize menu is available in the top-right corner. When working with Safari, you first have to enable the Developer Tools by opening Safari's **Preferences** panel and then selecting the **Show Develop** menu in the menu bar checkbox. You can then access the inspector by choosing **Show Web Inspector** from the application's **Develop** menu.

Since the Web Inspector is part of the WebKit codebase, you can use the same shortcuts in Chrome and Safari to access the debugging tools.

On Windows and Linux, press:

- *Ctrl + Shift + I* to open Developer Tools
- *Ctrl + Shift + J* to open Developer Tools and bring focus to the console
- *Ctrl + Shift + C* to toggle the Inspect Element mode

On OS X, press:

- ⌥ ⌘ I (option + command + I) to open Developer Tools
- ⌥ ⌘ J (option + command + J) to open Developer Tools and bring focus to the console
- ⌥ ⌘ C (option + command + C) to toggle the Inspect Element mode

When accessing Developer Tools, you can switch between tools by clicking on the respective icon.

The **Elements** panel allows you to see the webpage as the browser renders it. When using it, you can see the raw HTML and CSS, and explore the **Document Object Model** (**DOM**). By clicking on the **Elements** panel and moving around the source of the page, you can identify the HTML blocks and change the CSS selector's value on-the-fly in order to experiment and fix possible rendering issues:

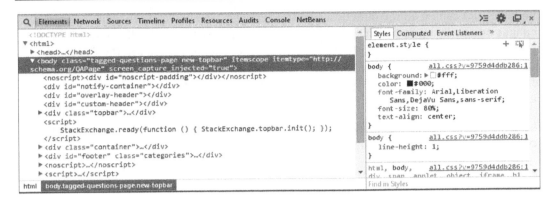

The **Resources** panel lets you inspect resources that are loaded and available in the inspected page. It lets you interact with frame trees containing frame resources (HTML, JavaScript, CSS, images, fonts, and so on), HTML5 databases, local storage, cookies, and AppCache.

Using the **Network** panel, you can explore the components that a webpage or application requests from web servers, how long these requests take, and how much bandwidth is required.

Using the **Sources** panel, you can access all the resources loaded into the page. Use this panel to access the JavaScript, set breakpoints in the code, and explore the stack trace for each error. In order to set a breakpoint, select the script in which you want to set the breakpoint, and then click on the line number you are interested in. When the debug tool reaches the breakpoint, you can see what's happening in your code by exploring the call stack (that is, the chain of functions and/or methods executed until this breakpoint) and the scope variables, and move in and out of functions:

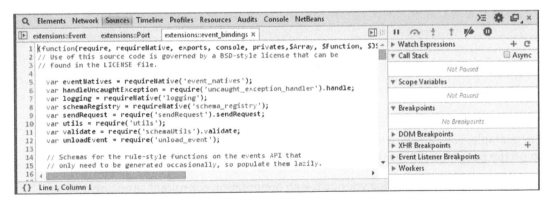

The JavaScript can be edited directly inside the debugger and you can see your changes on-the-fly by going back and forth using the navigation arrows. If you want the debugger to stop the code execution each time an exception is raised, use the **Pause all** button at the bottom left of the panel. For details about each of the functionalities, we recommend that you refer to the official docs at `https://developer.chrome.com/devtools/docs/javascript-debugging`.

The **Timeline** panel lets you analyze the various WebKit behind-the-scenes activities such as how long the browser takes to handle DOM events, render page layouts, and handle events.

Once you press the Record button, you can start to inspect what's happening in the page you are currently viewing.

The Events and Frames icons (available in Chrome) allow you to access two different timeline data views, the first one is based on time and the second one is based on frames; you can zoom into each view by using the grey vertical controls at the top.

The Memory icon lets you explore the memory usage of a specific webpage; in order to be more accurate during the exploration, it's a good habit to force the garbage collector by pressing the Trash icon at the bottom of the panel. Garbage collection is a form of automatic memory management; the collector attempts to reclaim garbage or memory occupied by objects that are no longer being used by the browser's window.

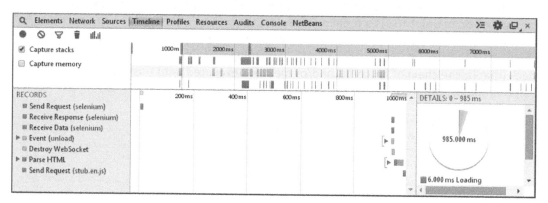

The **Profiles** tool helps you capture and analyze the performance of JavaScript scripts. For example, you can learn which functions take the most time to execute and then zoom in on the possible bottlenecks and understand exactly where to optimize.

The **Audits** panel is like having your own web optimization consultant sitting next to you. This panel can analyze a page as it loads and then provide suggestions and optimizations to decrease page load time and increase perceived responsiveness.

Gecko debugging – Firefox

Firefox is based on the Gecko open source layout engine used in many applications developed by the Mozilla Foundation and the Mozilla Corporation. It offers good debugging tools and it's evolving quickly, including innovative projects such as Desktop WebRT, which lets you build a desktop web application at runtime that provides web apps with a native-like look and feel along with platform integration APIs on Windows, OS X, and other desktop platforms.

If you are not developing apps for Android or iOS, you can use the Firefox layout engine, which offers some powerful development and debugging tools. Let's quickly explore how to use Firefox/Firebug to inspect and debug your app; as you will see, there are several similarities between the debug tools available in WebKit and Firefox.

Firebug integrated with Firefox puts a great set of developer tools at your fingertips that rivals the features of the WebKit Web Inspector. In order to install the Firebug extension, you have to go to `https://www.getfirebug.com/downloads/` and install the latest version. Once installed, you can open the extension by navigating to **Tools** | **Web Developer** | **Firebug**.

The Firebug toolbar gives you access to the HTML source code and CSS rules, lets you explore and debug JavaScript functions, and more:

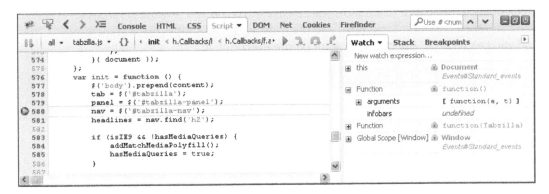

Once the debugger reaches a breakpoint, you can:

 ◆ Explore the variables defined in the block of code in which you set up the breakpoint

 ◆ Explore the stack of function/method calls

 ◆ Create watches in order to understand how the content of a variable changes during the execution of the code

The Script console in Firebug is amazing. You can type your code in to the right window and then run it and see the results in the console by clicking on the **Run** button at the bottom right of the panel:

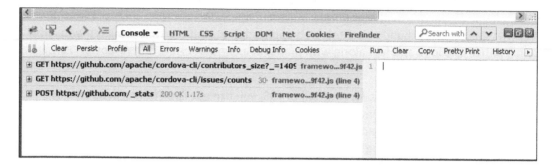

To filter logs, use the **All**, **Errors**, **Warnings**, **Info**, **Debug Info**, and **Cookies** selectors at the top of the window.

As mentioned previously, Firefox has three great native development tools: Scratchpad, Inspect, and Responsive Design View. You can access these tools through the menu bar by navigating to **Tools | Web Developer**.

Think of Scratchpad as a text editor; you can use it to type and execute JavaScript. The difference between Scratchpad and the console is that it looks like a text editor and you can write all the code you want before executing it:

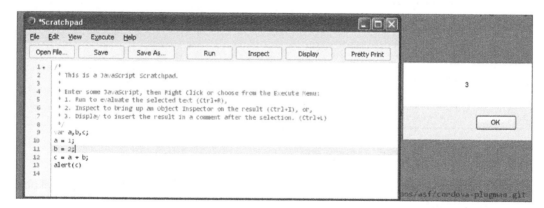

The Responsive Design View tool lets you change the resolution without resizing the browser. You can also use it to simulate device rotation:

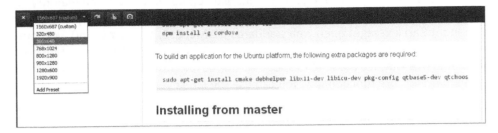

Internet Explorer

Internet Explorer, at the time of writing, still has a wide install base; it's also the least favorite browser among developers. Virtually every developer has experienced serious issues when optimizing a webpage for IE; this is due to the fact that IE diverges from web standards in significant areas, but things are changing and the preview of IE 10 is getting good scores in various tests. Internet Explorer 11 is even better for developers.

Developer Tools were introduced in Internet Explorer 8, and updated with new functionality in Internet Explorer 9. Developer Tools in Internet Explorer 10 add Web Worker debugging and support for multiple script sources.

You can access Developer Tools by pressing *F12* or by navigating to **Tools | Developer Tools** from the menu bar:

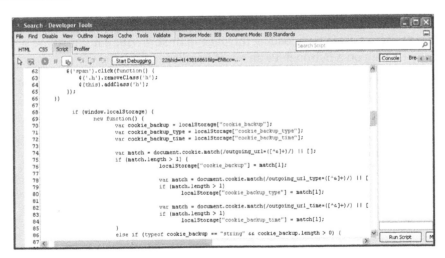

The IE 10 Developer Tools provide a similar user interface to the Developer Tools in Safari, Chrome, and Firefox.

Debugging workflow

The desktop browser is a great tool for hybrid mobile app development. The majority of your mobile development can be previewed and debugged in your desktop browser. Because PhoneGap leverages open web standards (HTML, CSS, and JavaScript), you can start work in a desktop browser and then move on to a native project once the functionality is fleshed out. This way, it's possible to speed up our development cycles and spend more time implementing core functionality. You can use the latest versions of any of the major desktop browsers such as Internet Explorer (IE), Google Chrome, Firefox, Safari, or Opera to get started with a PhoneGap app. All of these browsers have Developer Tools for logging and debugging your code.

New developers tend to prefer WebKit-based browsers; at the time of writing, Chrome has the largest install base market share followed by Firefox and Internet Explorer.

 Chrome also offers a technology known as **Google Packaged Apps** to build native apps based on web standards. More information about it is available at `https://developer.chrome.com/apps/about_apps`.

As you have seen, each browser offers different debugging tools and each tool has its pros and cons. Regardless of which tool you use, however, your debugging workflow is the same.

When investigating a specific problem, you will usually follow this process:

1. Find the relevant code in the debugger's code view pane.
2. Set breakpoint(s) where you think interesting things may occur.
3. Run the script again by reloading the page in the browser if it's an inline script, or by clicking on a button if it's an event handler.
4. Wait until the debugger pauses execution and makes it possible to step through the code.
5. Investigate the values of variables. For example, look for variables that are undefined when they should contain a value, or return `false` when you expect them to return `true`.

If necessary, you can use the console to evaluate code or change variables for testing. You can also execute complex JavaScript code and test a solution before implementing it.

Identifying the problem by learning which piece of code or input caused the error conditions and isolating it is a suitable approach. However, with mobile apps, things are not always so straightforward. The advantage of PhoneGap is that you can develop and debug in a common environment such as the browser, but keep in mind that a mobile app has to be tested and debugged on the target devices as well.

Although it's not a neat way of debugging, you can use console log messages to debug. These log messages will be printed in the console of the browser development tool. A sample use of the JavaScript code is provided here for reference:

```
console.log("Application running now");
```

There are several other debugging tools for PhoneGap/Cordova. While a few of them are free services, some of them are paid services:

1. **Ripple Emulator**: `http://emulate.phonegap.com/`
2. **GapDebug**: `https://www.genuitec.com/products/gapdebug/`
3. **jsHybugger**: `https://www.jshybugger.com/`
4. **Weinre**: `http://people.apache.org/~pmuellr/weinre-docs/latest/`
5. **Adobe Edge Inspect**: `https://creative.adobe.com/products/inspect`
6. **Chrome**: `https://developer.chrome.com/devtools/docs/remote-debugging`

Building and deployment

Once you are done with your development, you might want to test the application on a real mobile device. Each mobile platform will have a different kind of binary format for the applications. For example, Android application files will have the `.apk` extension. Similarly, each platform will have a different format for the application.

To create binary files for all platforms from your source code, you need to build the application either locally or by using a cloud service.

If you are building the application locally, you need to run the command-line interface, and the required platform's SDK should be installed on the machine. The CLI supports the following combinations on each operating system:

Windows	Linux	Mac
Amazon Fire OS	Amazon Fire OS	iOS (only on Mac)
Android	Android	
BlackBerry 10	BlackBerry 10	
Windows Phone 7	Firefox OS	
Windows Phone 8		
Windows 8		
Firefox OS		

This table makes it clear that you can't build an iOS application on a Windows machine or a Windows 8 application on a Mac machine. You will need an appropriate machine and the required SDKs installed on the machine.

Assuming you have all the required SDKs installed and configured, to build the application for each of the platform, you can use the **build** tool of CLI.

Run the following command to build the project for all the platforms added to the project. If you added multiple platforms to the project using the `platform add` command, the build will happen for all platforms:

```
C:\example1> phonegap build
```

If you want to build the application only for a particular platform, say Android or iOS, you can target them individually with the following commands:

```
C:\example1> phonegap build android
C:\example1> phonegap build ios
```

The `build` command is the shortcut to prepare and compile the project. You can also build a project in two steps, as shown here. The following set of commands is the equivalent of the `build` command:

```
C:\example1> phonegap prepare android
C:\example1> phonegap compile android
```

Once the build process is completed, the platform-specific app will be available within the project's `platforms` subdirectory.

Having seen the manual way of building an application, now let's find out about PhoneGap Build. If you want to build and generate application binary files for all platforms, you need to install the individual SDKs on your machine, which is not practically possible. That's where we find the PhoneGap Build process handy. PhoneGap Build is an online service for creating binary files for all mobile platforms based on a single source code.

It takes the source code and creates the app file for each of the platforms that you require. It's as simple as uploading your Cordova/PhoneGap project and the cloud service does the rest. The overall functionality of the PhoneGap Build process is provided in the following diagram, which is available at `https://build.phonegap.com`:

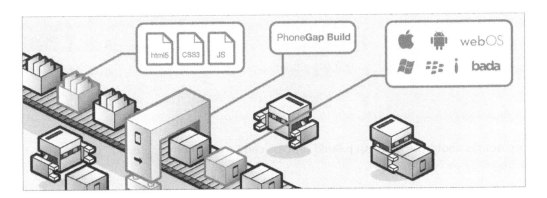

To use PhoneGap Build, you have to follow these steps:

1. Complete your PhoneGap/Cordova project and ensure you have all the functionalities included in the app as per your design.
2. PhoneGap Build only requires the contents (HTML, CSS, JavaScript, and images) of your project's `assets` directory.
3. If you have any `phonegap.js` or `cordova.js` files included in your assets, remove the file as the PhoneGap Build process will automatically inject the required file.
4. You can upload the project to the PhoneGap Build process and you can see the magic happen.

You can easily download all the application builds for all platforms with a single click:

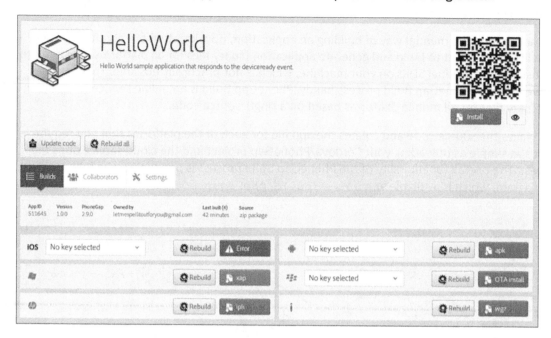

More details about the PhoneGap Build process can be obtained at `http://docs.build.phonegap.com/en_US/`.

Summary

After providing an overview of several tools and some debugging techniques, this chapter prepared you to move to the next step, creating and building a multi-platform app with Apache Cordova and its PhoneGap distribution. You also learned the usage of various command-line tools and Cordova events. In the next chapter, you'll gain information about various mobile frameworks and templates to start off your mobile development.

3
Mobile Frameworks

In Chapter 2, Building Your First PhoneGap Project, you learned about the PhoneGap app structure, events, how to use command-line tools, and how to create a sample app. You also learned about the various debugging methods that can help developers and saw how to build/deploy your app. In this chapter, you will learn about the design method, the mobile frameworks available in the industry, and the details regarding these. We will also see how to create a sample application using jQuery Mobile.

In this chapter, you will do the following things:

- ◆ Review some of the concepts on developing native UI for mobile
- ◆ Explore best practices for developing mobile UI
- ◆ Get an overview of the most popular app frameworks
- ◆ Learn how to create a mobile application using jQuery mobile

Building native UI for the mobile

When using PhoneGap, you create hybrid apps based on standards. The app is rendered to the user through a WebView, which means it is a browser instance wrapped into the app itself.

For this reason, it's important to know how to use mobile-specific HTML tags, CSS properties, and JavaScript methods, properties, and events.

The viewport meta tag

The `viewport` meta tag was introduced by Apple with iOS 1.0 and is largely supported in all the major mobile browsers. When a web page doesn't fit the size of the browser, the default behavior of a mobile browser is to scale it. The `viewport` meta tag is what you need in order to have control over this behavior.

A `viewport` meta tag looks like the following code snippet:

```
<meta name="viewport" content="width=device-width,
  height=device-height, initial-scale=1, minimum-scale=1,
  maximum-scale=1.5, user-scalable=1">
```

What you are actually saying to the browser is that the default width and height of the content are the width and height of the device screen (`width=device-width` and `height=device-height`), that the content is scalable (`user-scalable=1`), and what the minimum and maximum scale is (`minimum-scale=1` and `maximum-scale=1.5`).

An exhaustive reference covering the `viewport` meta tag is available on the Apple Developer Library website at `https://developer.apple.com/library/safari/#documentation/appleapplications/reference/SafariHTMLRef/Articles/MetaTags.html`. Some useful information is available on the Opera developer's website at `http://dev.opera.com/articles/view/an-introduction-to-meta-viewport-and-viewport/`.

Remember that by default the WebView used by PhoneGap ignores the settings defined in the `viewport` meta tag; you will learn during this chapter how to enable the handling of the viewport settings in your app.

Unwanted telephone number linking

The mobile browser click-to-call format detection on most phones isn't that accurate; plenty of numbers get selected, including addresses, ISBN numbers, and a variety of different types of numeric data that aren't phone numbers. In order to avoid any possible issues and to have full control on a call from your HTML markup, it is necessary to add the following meta tag to the header of your page:

```
<meta name="format-detection" content="telephone=no">
```

Defining this tag, you can then control how to handle numbers using the `tel` or `sms` scheme in the `href` attribute:

```
<a href="tel:18005555555">Call us at 1-800-555-5555</a>
<a href="sms:18005555555?body=Text%20goes%20here">
```

Please note that this telephone format detection will only work for mobile browsers. In desktop browsers, it does nothing, unless you have some desktop telephony software such as Skype installed on the desktop along with the browser plugin.

Autocorrect

Submitting data using mobile devices is a tedious operation for the user, because sometimes the built-in autocorrect features don't help at all. In order to disable the autocorrect features, use the `autocorrect`, `autocomplete`, and `autocapitalize` attributes in conjunction with an `input` field:

```
<input autocorrect="off" autocomplete="off" autocapitalize="off">
```

CSS media queries and mobile properties

One of the interesting features of CSS is media queries. Media queries themselves are actually quite old and not mobile-specific, but they are really useful when handling different screen sizes on mobiles. Media queries can be used inline:

```
@media all and (orientation: portrait) {
    body { }
    div { }
}
```

Alternatively, media queries can be used as the `media` attribute of a `link` tag:

```
<link rel="stylesheet" media="all and (orientation: portrait)"
  href="portrait.css" />
```

There is no best way to use them because it depends on the type of app. Using media queries inline, the CSS file tends to grow and the parsing can be slow on old devices. On the other hand, having CSS rules organized in separate files helps to keep the code well organized and speeds up the parsing, but it means more HTTP calls, which are usually not the best option on mobiles due to the latency of mobile connections.

A good balance should be reached using offline caching strategies, which you will learn more about in the next chapters.

There are several CSS mobile-specific properties; most of them are vendor-specific and are identified with prefixes. The most common properties used in mobile development are:

- `-webkit-tap-highlight-color: 0;` (iOS): This overrides the semitransparent color overlay when a user clicks on a link or clickable element. This is the only property that is iOS-specific.
- `-webkit-user-select: none;`: This prevents the user from selecting a text.
- `-webkit-touch-callout: none;`: This prevents the callout toolbar from appearing when a user touches and holds an element such as an `anchor` tag.

Always remember that the usage of browser prefixes in JavaScript is possible only by using mixed case or lower CamelCase formatting, which means that in order to prevent the user from selecting text through JavaScript, you have to use the following syntax:

```
yourElementVariable.style.webkitUserSelect = 'none';
```

The CamelCase formatting is due to the fact that the dash sign cannot be used in a variable name in JavaScript.

Screen orientation

The screen orientation is important when dealing with an app because the size of the screen dramatically changes when the orientation is changed. The `orientationchange` event is triggered at every 90 degrees of rotation (portrait and landscape modes), and it's possible to listen to it using `addEventListener`; the current orientation is available through `window.orientation`.

Device orientation

If you want to get more detailed information about the orientation of the device, you can define a listener for the `deviceorientation` event. The `deviceorientation` event will fire very frequently and give information about the device's orientation in three dimensions as values of alpha, beta, and gamma, as shown here:

```
window.addEventListener("deviceorientation", handleOrientation, true);

function handleOrientation(event) {
    var alpha    = event.alpha;
    var beta     = event.beta;
    var gamma    = event.gamma;

  // Change device orientation based on the data
}
```

The `deviceorientation` event is strictly related to the existence of a gyroscope on the device; the gyroscope measures the 3D angle orientation, even when the device is at rest. For details on using the orientation data, please refer to `https://developer.mozilla.org/en-US/docs/Web/API/Detecting_device_orientation`.

Shake gestures

Gesture handling is the key to successful apps. The `devicemotion` event fires when the user shakes or moves his/her device. The `devicemotion` event is strictly related to the accelerometer, which fires events off when the device accelerates.

Media capture APIs

While old versions of iOS are still lacking basic file input, Android, iOS version 6, and later, Windows Phone 8 and BlackBerry 10 are giving developers fine-grained control over content that users can upload and allow you to access the device camera and microphone:

```
<!-- opens directly to the camera -->
<input type="file" accept="image/*;capture=camera"></input>
<!-- opens directly to the camera in video mode -->
<input type="file" accept="video/*;capture=camcorder"></input>
<!-- opens directly to the audio recorder -->
<input type="file" accept="audio/*;capture=microphone"></input>
```

Data URI

You can represent an image as a Base64 string, which ensures higher performance because there is no TCP negotiation in order to open a new HTTP connection. Practically speaking, it means that there is a lower latency when compared to the usual way to load an image on the Web. When a `base64` string is assigned as the `src` attribute to an `img` tag, the code looks as shown in the following snippet:

```
<img src='data:image/png;base64,
R01GODlhEAAOALMAAOazToeHh0tLS/7LZv/0jvb29t/f3//Ub//
ge8WSLf/rhf/3kdbW1mxsbP//mf///
yH5BAAAAAAALAAAAAAQAA4AAARe8L1Ekyky67QZ1hLnjM5UUde0
ECwLJoExKcppV0aCcGCmTIHEIUEqjgaORCMxIC6e0CcguWw6aFj
sVMkkIr7g77ZKPJjPZqIyd7sJAgVGoEGv2xsBxqNgYPj/ gAwXEQA7' width='16'
height='14' >
```

When converting an image to Base64, there is a 30-40 percent weight increase; for this reason, you have to optimize the image carefully before converting it and when possible, activate GZip compression on the server.

Achieving a native look and feel on iOS

One of the biggest problems with the iOS platform is the publication of your app in the App Store. In fact, Apple is pretty scrupulous when checking whether an app can be added to the store.

One of the most important criteria to be admitted to the App Store is that the app provides an iOS user experience. For more details on the requirements an app must meet to make it into the App Store, go to the Apple Developer website available at `https://developer.apple.com/app-store/review/`.

In recent times, there have been several iOS-specific mobile frameworks developed, such as Framework 7, which can provide iOS native looks to your app. For more information, visit `http://www.idangero.us/framework7/`.

Choosing mobile frameworks

Developers typically have their own template libraries, built from scratch or commercial, to jump-start their projects. In this section, we will see a short overview of some useful HTML/CSS/JavaScript frameworks you can evaluate as your blueprint, libraries, and frameworks that you can integrate within your projects.

 A framework or a library is essentially a set of functions that you can call, these days usually organized into classes or files. A framework embodies some abstract design with more behavior built-in. Martin Fowler discusses further the difference between a library and a framework in his article available at `http://martinfowler.com/bliki/InversionOfControl.html`.

Using HTML5 Mobile Boilerplate

This is a very clean, mobile-friendly HTML template that includes an optimized Google Analytics snippet, placeholders for touch-based device icons, the library Zepto (a minimalist JavaScript library for modern browsers with a largely jQuery-compatible API), and the Modernizr feature detection library (a library that uses object detection techniques to discover whether a feature is available before you use it, allowing for graceful degradation or progressive enhancement of web pages).

You can download the HTML5 Mobile Boilerplate template from the official website at `http://html5boilerplate.com/mobile/`; for updates or to get involved, follow the project on GitHub at `https://github.com/h5bp/mobile-boilerplate`.

If you want to download a customized version of HTML5 Mobile Boilerplate, which enables you to select which templates to use, the JavaScript libraries to include, and so on, go to `http://www.initializr.com/`.

Using Zurb Foundation

You've probably already heard about responsive design, which is a website design that responds to the device constraints of the person viewing it. It's a hot topic right now and the Foundation framework's most important feature is the responsiveness of its layout mechanics.

Furthermore, Foundation provides a good selection of templates to use for the most common sections of your app; you can choose the templates you want when downloading the framework from `http://foundation.zurb.com/download.php`.

The strengths of Foundation are as follows:

- A 12-column, percentage-based grid with an arbitrary maximum width
- Image styles that disregard pixels—foundation images are scaled by the grid to different widths
- UI and layout elements, including common pieces such as typography and forms, as well as tabs, pagination, N-up grids, and more
- Mobile visibility classes—Foundation lets you very quickly hide and show elements on desktops, tablets, and phones

To keep up with Foundation and get the latest builds, follow the GitHub project available at `https://github.com/zurb/foundation`.

Using Twitter Bootstrap

Twitter Bootstrap is a free collection of tools used to create websites and web applications. It contains HTML- and CSS-based design templates for typography, forms, buttons, charts, navigation, and other interface components, as well as optional JavaScript extensions.

This project is one of the most popular on GitHub; it's very well organized and seems born to build apps. In fact, it includes basic CSS and HTML to create grids, layouts, typography, tables, forms, navigation, alerts, popovers, and so on.

It's pretty easy to start working with Bootstrap because it uses jQuery. To download Bootstrap, you can refer to the project download and customize page available at `http://twitter.github.com/bootstrap/customize.html`; if you want to download a template for Bootstrap, you can refer to the already mentioned `http://www.initializr.com/` website. But note that Bootstrap is specially designed for mobile web and not for hybrid mobile applications.

Ionic framework

Ionic framework is a powerful HTML5 hybrid app development framework that helps you build native-feeling mobile apps, all with web technologies such HTML, CSS, and JavaScript. It's made keeping hybrid mobile apps in mind. As Ionic is based on AngularJS and built on top of PhoneGap/Cordova CLI, you can see more CLI command syntax similar to it. It has a deep learning curve but it's worth learning. AngularJS is not a hybrid mobile framework by itself but Ionic gives everything that a hybrid mobile framework would need. The framework is actively maintained. Moreover, the framework handles UI rendering based on the platform to provide a native feel to the users. Note that it has official support only for Android and iOS. You can find more information from `http://ionicframework.com/`.

ExtJS

ExtJS is a JavaScript framework with good-looking UI widgets to build interactive websites, and Sencha Touch based on ExtJS can be used to build hybrid mobile applications. It has various features and it's hard to list them all. Also, overall, you will have all that you need to develop a feature-rich application. It has both open source license and enterprise license available and you can know more about it at `https://www.sencha.com/products/extjs/` and `https://www.sencha.com/products/touch`.

AngularJS

AngularJS is a JavaScript framework from Google and it's now the star of enterprise development. AngularJS and Cordova/PhoneGap gel very well as it's a framework based on JavaScript. AngularJS has steep learning curves, such as ExtJS, but once you go through that phase, you will feel wonderful. To build hybrid applications, AngularJS has a special mobile counterpart called Mobile AngularJS UI. You can learn more about AngularJS and Mobile AngularJS UI at `http://angularjs.org` and `http://mobileangularui.com`, respectively.

jQuery Mobile

The jQuery Mobile framework is a user interface system that works across all popular mobile device platforms, built on the rock-solid jQuery and jQuery UI foundation. Its codebase is built with progressive enhancement and has a flexible, easily themeable design.

jQuery Mobile has broad support for all the major modern desktop, smartphone, tablet, and e-reader platforms. In addition, feature phones and older browsers are supported because of the progressive enhancement approach (for details, go to `http://jquerymobile.com/gbs/`).

The main features of jQuery Mobile can be summarized as follows:

- Cross-platform, cross-device, and cross-browser
- UI optimized for touch devices
- Themeable and customizable design
- Usage of non-intrusive semantic HTML5 code only
- AJAX calls automatically load dynamic content
- Lightweight (12 KB compressed)
- Progressive enhancement
- Accessible

To download the last stable version and to keep up-to-date with the project, refer to the official website available at `http://jquerymobile.com`, where you can find useful examples and a tool to create your own themes at `http://jquerymobile.com/themeroller/`.

Time for action – developing with jQuery Mobile

Let's see a quick example of how to use jQuery Mobile in a PhoneGap application. You can make any HTML page mobile friendly by using jQuery Mobile. We will create a simple app to show multiple entries in the page as a list and show some footer menus.

1. To start with, we need to download jQuery and jQuery Mobile components and place them in our project's JS/CSS directory. jQuery is a single JavaScript file and jQuery Mobile includes both a JavaScript file and a CSS file. We need to include them both in our app's HTML page.

2. Include the CSS file at the top of the HTML page, right above the `</head>` tag:

    ```
    <link rel="stylesheet" href="css/jquery.mobile-1.4.4.min.css" />
    ```

3. Include the JavaScript files at the bottom of the page, right above the `</body>` tag:

    ```
    <script src="js/jquery-1.11.1.min.js"></script>
    <script src="js/jquery.mobile-1.4.4.min.js"></script>
    ```

4. In jQuery Mobile, you define a page section by assigning the `data-role` property to `page`.

    First, let's add a `div` element to mark a page:

    ```
    <div data-role="page">
    </div>
    ```

5. Now, let's add a list to the page. A list in jQuery Mobile is identified by adding a `listview` data role to the `<ul>` element:

    ```
    <div data-role="page">
        <ul data-role="listview">
        </ul>
    </div>
    ```

6. To add items to the list view, we will add data to the `<ul>` tag as shown here:

    ```
    <div data-role="page">
      <ul data-role="listview">
        <li><a href="#">Apache</a></li>
        <li><a href="#">BASIC</a></li>
        <li><a href="#">COBOL</a></li>
    ```

```
            <li><a href="#">Delphi</a></li>
            <li><a href="#">FOTRON</a></li>
            <li><a href="#">Hadoop</a></li>
            <li><a href="#">Java</a></li>
            <li><a href="#">PHP</a></li>
            <li><a href="#">Perl</a></li>
            <li><a href="#">Python</a></li>
            <li><a href="#">jQuery</a></li>
        </ul>
    </div>
```

You can test the output either in a desktop browser or in a mobile emulator from the IDEs. For the preceding code, you will see the following output in your emulator:

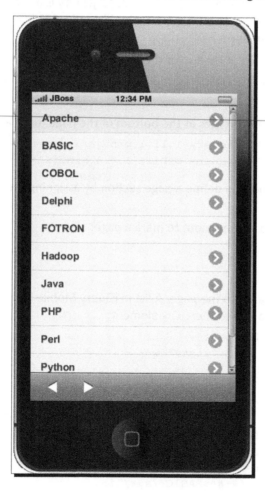

7. Now let's add a header to the page to make it look better. To add a header to the page, use the `data-role` attribute as `header`, as shown here:

```
<div data-role="header">
  <h1>Tech Words</h1>
</div>
```

With the header, you will now see the following output in the emulator:

8. Now, it's time to add a footer menu to the application. Use the following code to add a footer menu to the page:

```
<div data-role="navbar">
  <ul>
    <li><a href="#" data-icon="bars">Tools</a></li>
    <li><a href="#" data-icon="home">Languages</a></li>
    <li><a href="#" data-icon="search">Database</a></li>
  </ul>
</div>
```

The preceding HTML code creates a simple unordered list inside a `div` element. The content of the list will act as a navigation bar based on the `data-role` property we set.

Now the application will look as shown in the following screenshot:

We created a simple application based on jQuery Mobile and the complete `index.html` code is provided here for your reference:

```
<!DOCTYPE html>
<html>
<head>
<meta http-equiv="Content-Type" content="text/html; charset=UTF-8" />
<meta name="format-detection" content="telephone=no" />
<meta name="viewport"
  content="user-scalable=no, initial-scale=1, maximum-scale=1,
minimum-scale=1, width=device-width;" />
<link rel="stylesheet" href=" css/jquery.mobile-1.4.4.min.css" />
<title>Hello Cordova</title>
```

```
    </head>
    <body>
      <div data-role="page">
        <div data-role="header">
          <h1>Tech Words</h1>
        </div>
        <ul data-role="listview">
          <li><a href="#">Apache</a></li>
          <li><a href="#">BASIC</a></li>
          <li><a href="#">COBOL</a></li>
          <li><a href="#">Java</a></li>
          <li><a href="#">PHP</a></li>
          <li><a href="#">Perl</a></li>
          <li><a href="#">jQuery</a></li>
        </ul>
        <div data-role="navbar">
        <ul>
          <li><a href="#" data-icon="bars">Tools</a></li>
          <li><a href="#" data-icon="home">Languages</a></li>
          <li><a href="#" data-icon="search">Database</a></li>
        </ul>
        </div>
      </div>
      <script src=" js/jquery-1.11.1.min.js"></script>
      <script src=" js/jquery.mobile-1.4.4.min.js"></script>
    </body>
    </html>
```

Selecting a framework

It's pretty hard to say which is the best framework to use since each one has its own advantages and disadvantages. Most of the time, I have to say that it depends on the features you have to implement and even more so on the nature of your app. For instance, if the app is just for mobiles, then you can decide to go lighter and use HTML5 Mobile Boilerplate; on the other hand, if the app is intended for the Web and mobiles, then a more sophisticated library can be the right choice.

jQuery Mobile is pretty much easy and straightforward to learn and implement. However, when it comes to good performance, jQuery Mobile is not the leader. On the other hand, certain frameworks such as ExtJS and Ionic require more learning to use them in an enterprise-ready application. They have several ready-to-use components that help in rapid development.

Some of the frameworks are CSS only, some JavaScript and some with a mix of both. For example, jQuery Mobile provides both CSS theming capabilities and also JavaScript plugins to add more features. Always keep in mind that your goal is to find a balance between the built-in features and performance because mobile devices are far less powerful than a desktop.

Summary

In this chapter, you learned how to build a PhoneGap app that looks native on all platforms and got an overview of various mobile development frameworks. A sample jQuery Mobile application code was explained step-by-step. In the next chapter, you will learn how to work with plugins in your Cordova/PhoneGap project. You will find out how to install, integrate, and remove plugins using command-line tools.

4

Working with Plugins

Using web standards and JavaScript to build a native app may have its limitations, because apps developed using native code can interact deeply with the operating system. But this is only partially true when dealing with PhoneGap apps because its architecture allows developers to extend the framework capabilities with the help of custom plugins.

In this chapter you will:

◆ Learn what a PhoneGap plugin is and how to install the plugins in your project

◆ Know how to list all the installed plugins and remove unwanted plugins

◆ Understand how to manage project plugins and their dependencies using Plugman

◆ Discover how to implement the Device API in the project

An introduction to plugins

When you develop and deploy a new simple hybrid application, the application might not be doing anything advanced. We know hybrid applications are developed using standard web technologies such as HTML, CSS, and JavaScript. We need some mechanism for the application to interact with various device-level features. To achieve this, we use plugins with PhoneGap/Cordova APIs. Since version 3.0, all the PhoneGap APIs have been converted to plugins, which means having a deep understanding of the plugins is now even more important for a PhoneGap developer.

A PhoneGap plugin is a bridge between the WebView and the native platform on which the app is running.

In order to be productive quickly with PhoneGap plugins, it's important to keep in mind how the framework works. A PhoneGap app consists of three main layers. They are as follows:

- The user interface, developed using HTML, CSS, and JavaScript
- The business logic, developed in JavaScript
- The PhoneGap framework, native code exposed to the business logic through a JavaScript API

The user interface and the business logic are the app's main source code and the parts on which most developers concentrate their development efforts. The plugins are strictly integrated in the framework and are exposed to the user through JavaScript. You can imagine a plugin as an additional component of the framework that works similar to all the PhoneGap APIs.

Getting started with plugins

Using plugins you can extend the PhoneGap framework in order to meet the needs of your app. This means that there are no compelling limitations but it also means that the source code of your app has to be maintained for different platforms. There are several plugins listed for all platforms at `http://plugins.cordova.io`. In order to make sure that an existing plugin fits your needs, you have to double-check the compatibility with the PhoneGap version you are using in your project and eventually update the source code to be compliant. One of the strengths of PhoneGap is its continuous release model, because this speeds up the release of new features and bug fixing. But it also means that a plugin should be maintained in order to meet the deprecation policy of the framework. Refer to the online Wiki for updated information about upcoming deprecations at `http://wiki.apache.org/cordova/DeprecationPolicy`.

In order to use the features implemented in a custom plugin, you have to install it in your project. It's not an easy task to manually manage the plugins in a PhoneGap project; thankfully, there is a command-line tool that makes your life easier.

Installing plugins

You can install plugins to your project using the CLI tools of Cordova. The following command will add the plugin to your project and make the necessary changes to the manifest files if required:

```
$ cordova plugin add PLUGIN.ID
```

Here, `PLUGIN.ID` is the ID of the plugin as registered in the plugin repository.

The following list summarizes the currently available APIs and the commands to run to add them to a PhoneGap project. If you want to remove a plugin, use the $ cordova plugin remove command instead.

- Basic device information:
    - **Device API**: This gets basic information related to the device
      ```
      $ cordova plugin add cordova-plugin-device
      ```
    - **StatusBar API**: This customizes the status bar background
      ```
      $ cordova plugin add cordova-plugin-statusbar
      ```
- Network and battery status:
    - **Network API**: This gets cellular network information
      ```
      $ cordova plugin add cordova-plugin-network-information
      ```
    - **Battery API**: This monitors the status of the device's battery
      ```
      $ cordova plugin add cordova-plugin-battery-status
      ```
- Accelerometer, compass, and geolocation:
    - **Device Motion (Accelerometer) API**: This handles the device's motion sensor
      ```
      $ cordova plugin add cordova-plugin-device-motion
      ```
    - **Device Orientation API**: This gets the device orientation
      ```
      $ cordova plugin add cordova-plugin-device-orientation
      ```
    - **Geolocation API**: This makes the application location-aware
      ```
      $ cordova plugin add cordova-plugin-geolocation
      ```
- Camera, media capture, and media playback:
    - **Camera API**: This captures a photo using the device's camera
      ```
      $ cordova plugin add cordova-plugin-camera
      ```
    - **Capture API**: This captures all media files using the device
      ```
      $ cordova plugin add cordova-plugin-media-capture
      ```
    - **Media API**: This records and plays back audio files
      ```
      $ cordova plugin add cordova-plugin-media
      ```

- Access files on device or network:
  - **File API**: This accesses the filesystem of the device
    ```
    $ cordova plugin add cordova-plugin-file
    ```
  - **File Transfer API**: This uploads or downloads files using the API
    ```
    $ cordova plugin add cordova-plugin-file-transfer
    ```
- Notifications via dialog box or vibration:
  - **Dialogs API**: Using this, notifications and alerts are made easy
    ```
    $ cordova plugin add cordova-plugin-dialogs
    ```
  - **Vibration API**: This vibrates the device
    ```
    $ cordova plugin add cordova-plugin-vibration
    ```
- Contacts:
  - **Contacts API**: This gives complete access to the device's contact list
    ```
    $ cordova plugin add cordova-plugin-contacts
    ```
- Globalization:
  - **Globalization API**: This adds locale support to the application
    ```
    $ cordova plugin add cordova-plugin-globalization
    ```
- Splash screen:
  - **Splash screen API**: This shows and hides splash screen
    ```
    $ cordova plugin add cordova-plugin-splashscreen
    ```
- In-app browser:
  - **InApp Browser API**: This launches any URLs in an in-app browser
    ```
    $ cordova plugin add cordova-plugin-inappbrowser
    ```

Although the simplest way to add the plugin is to use the plugin ID, there are other advanced options as well. These options help us customize the plugin installation. Instead of using the plugin ID, we can use the GitHub repo URL as shown here:

```
$ cordova plugin add URL_TO_THE_GITHUB_REPO
```

Here, URL_TO_THE_GITHUB_REPO is the path to the plugin (that is, API) repository.

For example, you can install the Device API plugin in the following way:

```
$ cordova plugin add https://github.com/apache/cordova-plugin-device.git
```

Alternatively, you can install the Device API plugin this way as well:

```
$ cordova plugin add cordova-plugin-device
```

If you are using PhoneGap CLI instead of Cordova CLI, you can use either of the following two commands provided here. The following example command installs the Camera plugin to your project.

```
$ phonegap plugin add https://github.com/apache/cordova-plugin-camera.git
```

Alternatively, you can use the following command:

```
$ phonegap plugin add cordova-plugin-camera
```

If you would like to install a particular version of the plugin, you can specify it along with the plugin ID:

```
$ cordova plugin add cordova-plugin-camera@0.3.6
```

If you want to install a plugin from a local directory source, you can use the following format where you can specify the path to the source instead of the GIT repository URL:

```
cordova plugin add /path/to/directory
```

PhoneGap will look in this directory and each of its subdirectories for the plugin.

Listing installed plugins

To list all the plugins installed in the application project, you can use the `list` command. It has three variations and all will output the same:

```
$ cordova plugin
$ cordova plugin list
$ cordova plugin ls
```

All the preceding three commands will list the plugins installed along with the plugin ID, version, and the full name.

Removing plugins

Sometimes you may need to remove a plugin that you no longer want to use in your application. As with adding a plugin, removing a plugin is also simple. To remove a plugin, refer to it by the same plugin ID that appears in the listing. For example, here is how you would remove support for the Camera API from the project:

```
$ cordova plugin rm cordova-plugin-camera
```

Alternatively, you can use this command for the same:

```
$ cordova plugin remove cordova-plugin-camera
```

If you want to remove more than one plugin at a time, you can specify more than one argument:

```
$ cordova plugin rm cordova-plugin-console cordova-plugin-camera
```

Using plugins with Plugman

Plugins are installed and removed using a tool called **Plugman**; from a developer's point of view, this is just a command available in the `cordova-cli` utility. The Apache Cordova Plugman project `http://github.com/apache/cordova-plugman` is an open source command-line utility distributed as an npm module to facilitate the installation and uninstallation of plugins. Plugman supports the Android, Amazon FireOS, BlackBerry 10, Windows Phone 8, and iOS platforms. The installation process is the same as any other npm module; remember that if you install it globally (using the `-g` option), you have to run the command as root:

```
$ npm install plugman -g
```

Once installed, you can use the following several commands from your command-line tool to get the source code of a plugin, install and uninstall it, and package the plugin to be distributed with your app (Plugman is part of the `cordova-cli` tool; you don't have to install it if you are already using it):

- The `--fetch` option retrieves a plugin from a directory, a Git repository, or by name, into the specified plugins directory:

  ```
  $ plugman --fetch https://github.com/phonegap-build/GAPlugin.git
  --plugins_dir PATH_TO_YOUR_PLUGINS_DIR
  ```

- The `--install` option installs a plugin for a specific target platform in a PhoneGap project. The plugin can be installed by name or by URL:

  ```
  $ plugman --platform PLATFORM --project PLATFORM_PROJECT_PATH
  --plugin https://github.com/phonegap-build/GAPlugin.git
  ```

> The `--plugin` argument can be the name of the plugin or the path to a Git repository. By default, Plugman launches the `install` command and fetches the plugin if it doesn't exist in the `plugins` directory. For this reason the `--install` argument is optional.

- The `--uninstall` option uninstalls a previously installed plugin by name:

  ```
  $ plugman --uninstall --platform PLATFORM --project PLATFORM_
  PROJECT_PATH --plugin PLUGIN_NAME
  ```

- The `--list` option lists all the plugins previously fetched using Plugman.

- The `--prepare` option sets up the plugin, properly injecting the JavaScript files needed and defining the appropriate permissions. The `--prepare` command is implicitly called when you install or uninstall a plugin.

The keyword `PLATFORM` can have any of these values: `ios`, `android`, `amazon-fireos`, `blackberry10`, or `wp8`. Also note that Plugman is a lower-level CLI and hence you can add the plugins only for one platform at a given time. If there are multiple targeted platforms, you need to use the Plugman CLI to install the plugin for each of those platforms. However, if you use the Cordova CLI to install the plugins, it will install the plugins for all targeted platforms at once.

In order to add the plugin to a target platform, you can run the `compile` command or the `prepare` command.

When using Plugman as a standalone utility, you can specify variables at install time using the `--variable` argument. Such variables are necessary for plugins requiring API keys or other custom, user-defined parameters.

To get the entire list of Plugman commands and their syntax, you can use the global `help` command as shown here:

```
plugman - help
```

Since the release of PhoneGap 3.0, all the APIs are available as external plugins; you will learn more about plugins later in this book. At this point, all you need to know is that treating each single API as a plugin allows you to compose a version of PhoneGap suited to your project needs.

Exploring the Device API

Since we have covered the basics of using plugins in a Cordova/PhoneGap project, we will now look at an example of how to use the Device plugin.

Device API is one of the simplest APIs of PhoneGap/Cordova, which provides you with details about the device on which it's running. This is a great API to try when you first learn about plugins. Using the API, you can get the following properties of the device:

- Device platform
- Device unique ID
- Device version number
- Device model name

You can use these properties to provide device-specific features to the users.

Time for action – accessing the Device API

You already used the deviceready event in *Chapter 2, Building Your First PhoneGap Project*, to handle the bootstrap of our app. Use the device API to get information about the type of device you are running once the event is fired.

1. Open the command-line tool and create a new Cordova project using the Cordova command-line utility you installed before:

```
$ cordova create DeviceApi
```

This will create a new directory called DeviceApi in your current working directory.

2. Move to the directory you just created:

```
$ cd DeviceAPI
```

3. Add the platforms you want to test on the device API. For example, we add the Android platform:

```
$ cordova platform add android
```

4. Install the device API plugin. You can also use the shortest way to install the plugin, as shown here, instead of using the entire GIT repository URL:

```
$ cordova plugin add cordova-plugin-device
```

5. In the www folder inside the project folder you just created, open the index.html file and add a div element with id to render the device information that will be gathered using the PhoneGap API:

```
<div id='deviceInfo'>Loading device properties...</div>
```

6. Define a listener for the deviceready event in order to access all the supported API properties:

```
document.addEventListener("deviceready", onDeviceReady, false);
```

7. Show the device information on the HTML page:

```
function onDeviceReady() {
  var element = document.getElementById('deviceInfo');

  element.innerHTML = 'Device Model: '  + device.model +
    '<br />' +
                      'Device Cordova: '  + device.cordova  +
    '<br />' +
                      'Device Platform: '  + device.platform +
    '<br />' +
                      'Device UUID: '      + device.uuid +
    '<br />' +
                      'Device Version: '  + device.version  +
    '<br />';
}
```

8. Build the project using the Cordova command-line utility:

```
$ cordova build
```

9. View the application in the emulator by using the following command. It might take some time to start the emulator:

```
$ cordova run
```

The entire code has been provided here for your reference:

```
<!DOCTYPE html>
<html>
<head>
<meta http-equiv="Content-Type" content="text/html; charset=UTF-8" />
<meta name="format-detection" content="telephone=no" />
<meta name="viewport" content="user-scalable=no, initial-scale=1,
maximum-scale=1, minimum-scale=1, width=device-width;" />
<title>Hello Cordova</title>
</head>
<body>
<div id='deviceInfo'>Loading device properties...</div>

<script type="text/javascript" src="cordova.js"></script>
<script type="text/javascript">
        document.addEventListener('deviceready', onDeviceReady,
false);

        function onDeviceReady() {
            var element = document.getElementById('deviceInfo');
```

```
                    element.innerHTML = 'Device Model: ' +  device.model   +
                       '<br />'  +  'Device Cordova: '  +  device.cordova   +
                       '<br />'  +  'Device Platform: '  +  device.platform  +
                       '<br />'  +  'Device UUID: '    +  device.uuid  +
                       '<br />'  + 'Device Version: '  + device.version  +
                       '<br />';

            }
            </script>
        </body>
        </html>
```

This is how the output is going to look on the actual device. The values that you see on your actual device might vary depending on your device:

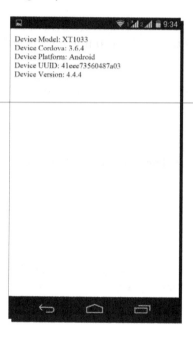

What just happened?

You handled the `deviceready` event, accessing the relevant device information using the PhoneGap API. The device object you just used describes the device's hardware and software:

◆ `device.platform`: This gets the operating system name

◆ `device.uuid`: This gets the Universally Unique Identifier

- device.version: This gets the operating system version
- device.cordova: This gets the version of Cordova running on the device
- device.model: This gets the model name

 Due to the rolling release model of PhoneGap, it's strongly suggested that you always refer to the GitHub repository at https://github.com/apache/cordova-plugin-device in order to check whether a specific device API is going to be deprecated.

Custom plugins

We saw the list of basic plugins available for Cordova/PhoneGap platforms and how to use them in our application. The developer is not limited to use only these small set of plugins. There are several hundreds of plugins available and many new plugins are added every day. Here are some of the most used third-party plugins. You should be careful on selecting the plugins based on their support for various platforms.

- **Social Sharing**: This adds social sharing features to your application (http://plugreg.com/plugin/EddyVerbruggen/SocialSharing-PhoneGap-Plugin)
- **Push Notifications**: This sends custom push notifications to your users (http://plugreg.com/plugin/phonegap-build/PushPlugin)
- **Facebook Login**: This enables users to log in to your application using Facebook (http://plugreg.com/plugin/Wizcorp/phonegap-facebook-plugin)
- **ActionSheet**: This shows wonderful action sheet menus in your application (http://plugreg.com/plugin/EddyVerbruggen/cordova-plugin-actionsheet)
- **AppRate**: This enables your users to add their feedback and rating for your application in the Google Play Store, Apple App Store, or in Windows Store (http://plugreg.com/plugin/pushandplay/cordova-plugin-apprate)

You can install these plugins either from their GitHub URL or using their plugin ID if registered in the Cordova plugin's repository. Here are the two methods to install the Social Sharing plugin. You can use this command:

```
$ cordova plugin add https://github.com/EddyVerbruggen/SocialSharing-PhoneGap-Plugin.git
```

You can also use this command:

```
$ cordova plugin add nl.x-services.plugins.socialsharing
```

For the complete list of plugins, you can refer to `http://plugins.cordova.io` or `http://plugreg.com`.

Summary

In this chapter, you learned about plugins and how to list, add, and remove them from the application. Using these techniques, we saw how to install the Device API in your project and get the details of the device. In the coming chapters, we will see how to access the local device storage using the Storage API and how to list/read/write files using the File API.

5
Using Device Storage and the Files API

Your knowledge of PhoneGap is coming together well. It's time to add some interaction with external data sources and with the device itself. The main goal of this chapter is to guide you through the offline storage capabilities of PhoneGap and help you understand how to interact with the Files API.

In this chapter, you will:

- Learn how to read and write data on the device using the `localStorage` object
- Learn how to handle the storage on a local database considering the specific platform implementation
- Understand database storage limitations and learn how to handle them
- Learn about the Files API, how it works, and how to organize your code to keep it clear and maintainable
- Use the Files API to explore the device filesystem
- Learn how to read and render data inside a file
- Learn how to load and save a file to a device's persistent storage

Application data storage

Every application (desktop, web, or mobile) needs to store (and access) some data in order to work properly. How the data is stored depends on the kind of information the application will work with and on the environment in which the application will run. A web application, for instance, can rely mostly on server storage because it runs on the Internet. Most advanced web applications implement an offline strategy and store some data locally on the user machine.

Modern web development offers several tools in order to let users interact with an application even when they're not connected:

- The **LocalStorage** API (http://www.w3.org/TR/webstorage/#the-localstorage-attribute)
- The **SessionStorage** API (http://www.w3.org/TR/webstorage/#the-sessionstorage-attribute)
- The **ApplicationCache** interface (http://www.w3.org/TR/2011/WD-html5-20110525/offline.html)
- The **IndexedDB** API (http://www.w3.org/TR/IndexedDB/)

All the modern mobile browsers let developers handle the online and offline events through the navigator object (https://developer.mozilla.org/en/docs/Online_and_offline_events).

 It's important to keep in mind that the specifications about the OnLine attribute report that this attribute is inherently unreliable because a computer can be connected to a network without having Internet access.

A complete overview of the previous API, events, and interface is beyond the scope of this book. In the following sections, I will discuss only those that are most relevant for building a PhoneGap app: LocalStorage and IndexedDB.

Exploring the PhoneGap LocalStorage API

There are two main web storage types: **local storage** and **session storage**. The LocalStorage API is part of the **WebStorage** API defined by the W3C in order to provide a guideline for persistent data storage of key-value pair data in web clients. The LocalStorage API is designed to support data that needs to be available between sessions. In other words, the data your app saves when using the LocalStorage API will be available again the next time the app runs.

In order to access the LocalStorage API, you have to refer the `window` object to its `localStorage` property. If you type the following snippet in your browser console, you can take a look at the methods and properties of the `localStorage` object:

```
console.log(window.localStorage);
```

The following list summarizes the available methods and properties:

- `key`: This returns the key name stored at a specific position; you can access the `localStorage` data either by key or by index
- `getItem`: This returns the value identified by a key
- `setItem`: This saves the value in a specific key (that is, a string) of the `localStorage` object; the method needs a string as a key and a value to store in the specific key
- `removeItem`: This removes the item identified by a key from the `localStorage` object
- `clear`: This removes all of the key-value pairs from the `localStorage` object
- `length`: This returns the total number of items stored in the `localStorage` object

The `localStorage` object allows you to store only simple string data as key-value pairs. If you want to store more complex data, you have to use JSON or other string representations of the data you want to store. When you use a JSON formatted string to store the value, you will need to convert the string back to JSON when you want to use it. Each time the `localStorage` object is updated, `StorageEvent` is fired. This event cannot be cancelled and contains the following properties:

- `key`: This is a string that represents the named key that was added, removed, or modified in the storage
- `oldValue`: This is the previous value of the named key if it was updated or null if a new item was added to the `localStorage` object
- `newValue`: This is the new value of the key or null if an item was removed
- `url`: This is the address of the HTML page that called a method that triggered this data change

 A JavaScript event is cancelable if it is possible to prevent the event's default action.

Keep in mind that storage events don't work for the same window or tab; they are fired only for other windows or tabs that use the same `localStorage` object.

The `localStorage` capabilities of PhoneGap allow you as a developer to write code as in the browser; it's the framework that handles the different platforms (Android, BlackBerry WebWorks OS 6.0 and higher, iOS, Windows Phone 7 and 8, and Tizen) on your behalf.

There are some drawbacks when using the `localStorage` object. As the `localStorage` API is synchronous, the time required to access the `localStorage` object is greater than the time needed to access an object in memory. Due to this, the app might appear less responsive. Also, as already mentioned, complex data needs to be serialized and de-serialized. This process might further impact the responsiveness of the app. You can use JavaScript **WebWorker** to avoid any performance degradation, but the support depends on the platform browser implementation and not on PhoneGap.

These drawbacks, however, should not prevent you from using the LocalStorage API because, as with most performance metrics, these performance hits really matter when you perform the same operation multiple times in a row. More specifically, the performance degradation due to the time needed to access the `localStorage` object happens when different tabs/windows access the same object.

When the mobile app built on top of PhoneGap is running, it's almost impossible that `localStorage` is accessed at the same time by other tabs/windows (you should have an issue only if your app starts to use several `InAppBrowser` instances in `UIWebView` of the app).

We will create a sample app now to get familiarized with using the `localStorage` object and all the methods supported by it.

Time for action – reading and writing data on the LocalStorage

1. Open the command-line tool and create a new PhoneGap project using the PhoneGap CLI you installed before. This will create a new directory called `DeviceApi` in your current working directory; this can be done using the following command:

   ```
   $ phonegap create DeviceApi
   ```

2. Move to the directory you just created:

   ```
   $ cd DeviceApi
   ```

3. Add the platforms you want to test on the device API. For this example, we add the Android platform:

   ```
   $ cordova platform add android
   ```

4. Delete all the files and subdirectories except index.html inside the www directory. Open the index.html file you will find in the www root folder and add the following HTML code snippet:

```
<button type="button" onclick="addCountry()">Add Canada</button>
<br/><br/>
<button type="button" onclick="get1Data()">Get USA Data</button>
<br/><br/>
<button type="button" onclick="getAllData()">Get All Data</button>
<br/><br/>
<button type="button" onclick="removeAllData()">Remove All
Countries</button> <br/><br/>
```

This code will add four buttons, which will add new localStorage data, remove data, retrieve data, and clear all localStorage data. Note that each button has an onclick event referring to a function.

5. Now let's add the required JavaScript to the page. First, we will bind the onDeviceReady function to the deviceready event. This function is going to add 3 localStorage data when the page loads. The setItem method of the localStorage object is used to add a new key-value pair. This is shown here:

```
document.addEventListener("deviceready", onDeviceReady, false);

function onDeviceReady() {
        localStorage.setItem("IN", "India");
        localStorage.setItem("FR", "France");
        localStorage.setItem("USA", "U.S.A");
}
```

6. When the user clicks on the **Add Canada** button, we will need to add a new country to the localStorage object. We will use the setItem again to add the new item. Once done, we will display an alert. Note that you can't add the same key again to the storage, as shown here:

```
function addCountry() {
    localStorage.setItem("CA", "Canada");
    alert("Canada added successfully");
}
```

7. Now, to get a particular object from the storage, we should use the getItem method. When there is a matching key, the value is returned. If not, null is returned. In this example, we will get the value for the USA key and display it in the alert:

```
function get1Data() {
    var usa = localStorage.getItem("USA");
    alert("Country Name is " + usa);
}
```

8. To get all items from the storage, we should loop the `localStorage` object and get the keys one by one as shown in the following code:

```
function getAllData() {

    for(var i in localStorage){
        alert(localStorage.getItem(i));
    }


}
```

9. The `clear` method is used to clear out all the values from `localStorage` of the app:

```
function removeAllData() {
    window.localStorage.clear();
    alert("All Countries removed successfully");
}
```

As shown in the `removeAllData` function, we can use `window.localStorage` instead of `localStorage` to work with the `localStorage` object.

The complete code for this example is provided for your reference as follows:

```
<!DOCTYPE html>
<html>
    <head>
        <!--Other section removed for sake of simplicity -->
        <title>Hello World</title>
    </head>
<body>
<button type="button" onclick="addCountry()">Add Canada</button>
<br/><br/>
<button type="button" onclick="get1Data()">Get USA Data</button>
<br/><br/>
<button type="button" onclick="getAllData()">Get All Data</button>
<br/><br/>
<button type="button" onclick="removeAllData()">Remove All Countries</button> <br/><br/>

<script type="text/javascript" src="cordova.js"></script>
<script type="text/javascript">
document.addEventListener("deviceready", onDeviceReady, false);
```

```
function onDeviceReady() {
    localStorage.setItem("IN", "India");
    localStorage.setItem("FR", "France");
    localStorage.setItem("USA", "U.S.A");
}

function addCountry() {
    localStorage.setItem("CA", "Canada");
    alert("Canada added successfully");
}

function get1Data() {
    var usa = localStorage.getItem("USA");
    alert("Country Name is " + usa);
}

function getAllData() {
   for(var i in localStorage){
       alert(localStorage.getItem(i));
   }
}

function removeAllData() {
    window.localStorage.clear();
    alert("All Countries removed successfully");
}

</script>
</body>
</html>
```

What just happened?

You saved persistent data on the device using JavaScript that can also run in all major
desktop browsers. Keep in mind that each platform stores this data in a different location
and that this data may be cleared by the device. Depending on the platform, this data can be
deleted when the app is closed or when the device is rebooted. For this reason, it's strongly
encouraged not to use the localStorage object to store crucial information.

Exploring the PhoneGap SQL storage

The client-side storage implementation in different browsers on mobiles is pretty inconsistent right now. It's important to make an analysis of each browser implementation when working on a PhoneGap project because the app is rendered through WebView; on iOS, this is the Objective-C `UIWebView` class; on Android, it is `android.webkit.WebView`, and it differs on all other supported platforms. The web view simply exposes the underlying platform browser. For this reason, it's important to know which client-side storage option is supported by the mobile browsers of your target platform.

The following table summarizes the storage support for the mobile versions of the major browsers at the time of writing; the X sign indicates whether the feature is supported.

	Android browser	Firefox OS	iOS Safari	IE 11 Mobile	Chrome for Android
IndexedDB	X	X	X	X	X
Web SQL	X	---	X	---	X

IndexedDB is a simple flat-file database with hierarchical key-value persistence and basic indexing. **Web SQL** Is basically **SQLite** embedded in the browser. SQLite is a relational database contained in a small (approximately 350 KB) library written in C that is used by software such as **Skype** or **Photoshop Lightroom**. The main difference between these storage options is that IndexedDB is a NoSQL database that lets you work with your JavaScript objects and indexes based on your application needs, while Web SQL is a real, relational client-side database implementation. One of the advantages of using Web SQL is that you can share the same queries between the backend and frontend. When running some tests, you can see how much faster Web SQL can be.

 In order to run the same test on your machine, you can clone the GitHub repository at `https://github.com/scaljeri/indexeddb-vs-websql` and open the file `test.html` in your web browser.

The W3C dropped support for Web SQL on November 18, 2010, making IndexedDB the *de facto* standard. From a developer's point of view, IndexedDB may look like a huge step backward but it really isn't. For years, developers have stored data on the client side using key-value pairs, and most of the time they use JSON to query the objects using **Unstructured Query Language (UQL)** or NoSQL. For these reasons, IndexedDB should be seen as the natural evolution of client-side storage.

PhoneGap provides storage API based on the deprecated Web SQL database specification. When Web SQL is supported by the device, the app will use it. If not, the app will use the PhoneGap one. There will be no difference for the developer as we will not have to change any line of code.

Working with database storage in PhoneGap

To work with a `Database` object in PhoneGap, it's enough to use the `openDatabase` method shown as follows:

```
var size = (1024 * 1024 * 2);
var db = window.openDatabase("name", "1.0", "Test DB", size);
```

The `openDatabase` method accepts the following four (self-explanatory) arguments:

- The database **name**
- The database **version**
- The **display name** of the database
- Estimated **size** of the database

Keep in mind that an application can query the version number of the database in order to understand whether an upgrade to the database schema is required. The `openDatabase` method returns a reference to the currently open database.

In the previous snippet, I allocated 2 MB of space in bytes. When allocating space, consider that mobile devices may have limitations on the size of the database they can support. For example, iOS only allows up to 5 MB for web-based applications; the same is true when using PhoneGap as a wrapper.

The returned database object between the others exposes two methods that take from one to three arguments: `transaction()` and `readTransaction()`. The main difference is that the `readTransaction()` method has to be used in read-only mode. The arguments that can be passed to these methods are:

- A function to execute one or more SQL statements
- A function to handle an exception raised by the app when opening the database
- A function to handle the successful opening of the database

Note that the `transaction()` and `readTransaction()` asynchronous methods are the only methods in the PhoneGap framework that want the failure handler function before the success one. Also, the success handler is the only one that doesn't receive any argument; the other handlers receive a `SQLTransaction` object.

The SQLTransaction object exposes the executeSql method. Using this method, it's possible to run several SQL statements and pass some parameters to the statements to handle successful SQL query execution and SQL errors.

> You can use several tokens in order to pass parameters to a SQL statement. For a complete overview of the available tokens, refer to the online documentation at http://www.sqlite.org/lang_expr.html.

The success handler receives two arguments: the first one is a reference to the transaction itself and the second one is a SQLResultSet object that contains the information, and optionally the results, of the executed query.

> The insertId property of the SQLResultSet object returns an Exception: DOMException value when performing a SELECT statement. You can safely ignore it because it doesn't affect the app.

Time for action – populating a local database

In order to reinforce what you just learned, you will create a new local database, add a table to it, and write and read some data.

1. Return to the project you created for the previous example or create a new project. Clean out the content of the index.html file, and add the following button markup to it. This button will be used to query the data back from the database:

```
<button type="button" onclick="queryEmployees()">Fetch All
  Rows</button>
```

2. Create a JavaScript tag and the deviceready event listener:

```
document.addEventListener("deviceready", onDeviceReady, false);
```

3. In the body of the onDeviceReady function, we will create a new database called EMP with version number of 1.0, named Employee Details, with an estimated size of 2 MB:

```
var size = (1024 * 1024 * 2);

function onDeviceReady() {
    var database = window.openDatabase('employee', '1.0',
      'Employee Details', size);
    database.transaction(populateDB, onError, onSuccess);
}
```

Once the database is created using the `openDatabase` method, we populate the database. We have to create a transaction for every operation we need to perform and so we provide the `populateDB` method as an argument for the transaction:

```
function populateDB(tx) {
    tx.executeSql('DROP TABLE IF EXISTS EMP');
    tx.executeSql('CREATE TABLE IF NOT EXISTS EMP (id unique,
      name)');
    tx.executeSql('INSERT INTO EMP (id, name) VALUES (1, "John
      Doe")');
    tx.executeSql('INSERT INTO EMP (id, name) VALUES (2, "Jane
      Doe")');
}

function onError(err) {
    alert("SQL Error: " + err.code);
}

function onSuccess() {
    alert("Success!");
}
```

The `executeSql` method can take any standard SQL statement and execute it.

4. We will now create the `queryEmployees` function, which is bound to the button `onclick` event. This function is going to open the database and create a transaction to query the database:

```
function queryEmployees() {
    var database = window.openDatabase('employee', '1.0',
      'Employee Details', size);
    database.transaction(queryData, onError);
}
```

5. The `queryData` function provided as an argument to the transaction executes the SQL query. This takes the transaction argument `tx` and the result set is passed to the `onSelectSuccess` function:

```
function queryData(tx) {
    tx.executeSql('SELECT * FROM EMP', [], onSelectSuccess,
      onError);
}
```

6. The onSelectSuccess function has the transaction and result set as an argument and does the actual parsing job:

```
function onSelectSuccess(tx, results) {

    var len = results.rows.length;
    alert("Total Employees : " + len);

    for (var i=0; i<len; i++){
        alert(results.rows.item(i).id + " - "
               + results.rows.item(i).name);
    }
}
```

The complete code of this example is provided for your quick reference. You can also verify the database records in your browser developer tools:

```
<!DOCTYPE html>
<html>
    <head>
        <!--Other section removed for sake of simplicity -->
        <title>Database Example</title>
    </head>
<body>
    <button type="button" onclick="queryEmployees()">Fetch All
      Rows</button>
    <script type="text/javascript" src="cordova.js"></script>

    <script type="text/javascript">
        var size = (1024 * 1024 * 2);

        document.addEventListener("deviceready", onDeviceReady, false);

        function onDeviceReady() {
          var database = window.openDatabase('employee', '1.0',
            'Employee Details', size);
          database.transaction(populateDB, onError, onSuccess);
        }

        function populateDB(tx) {
          tx.executeSql('DROP TABLE IF EXISTS EMP');
          tx.executeSql('CREATE TABLE IF NOT EXISTS EMP (id unique,
            name)');
```

```
      tx.executeSql('INSERT INTO EMP (id, name) VALUES (1, "John
        Doe")');
      tx.executeSql('INSERT INTO EMP (id, name) VALUES (2, "Jane
        Doe")');
    }

    function onError(err) {
      alert("SQL Error: " + err.code);
    }

    function onSuccess() {
      alert("Success!");
    }

    function queryEmployees() {
      var database = window.openDatabase('employee', '1.0',
        'Employee Details', size);
      database.transaction(queryData, onError);
    }

    function queryData(tx) {
      tx.executeSql('SELECT * FROM EMP', [], onSelectSuccess,
        onError);
    }

    function onSelectSuccess(tx, results) {

      var len = results.rows.length;
      alert("Total Employees : " + len);

      for (var i=0; i<len; i++){
        alert(results.rows.item(i).id + " - " + results.
          rows.item(i).name);
      }
    }
  </script>
</body>
</html>
```

What just happened?

You created a local database in order to store and recover information relevant for your app and its users. The database will be automatically removed when the app is uninstalled.

Database limitations

There are some limitations to be aware of when using the WebSQL implementation of PhoneGap (refer to the SQLite documentation for a complete overview at `http://www.sqlite.org/limits.html`). These limitations are not related to the framework itself but are due to the web view implementation of each target platform.

The limit you can easily hit when working on an app is the size limit of the database file. For example, on WebKit, it varies depending on the operating system from 5 MB to 25 MB. Another limitation you can find is that, since iOS 5.1, both `localStorage` and Web SQL databases have been moved to the `~/Library/Caches` folder from the `~/Library/WebKit` folder. Actually, this change means that the information stored is not backed up anymore and can be arbitrarily deleted by the operating system when more space is needed (for more information about iOS data management, refer to the Apple Developer guide at `https://developer.apple.com/technologies/ios/data-management.html`).

In order to avoid the issues described, you can use the Sqlite plugin available on GitHub for Android and iOS (`https://github.com/litehelpers/Cordova-sqlite-storage`).

 You will learn more about PhoneGap plugins throughout this book; for now, it suffices to know that a plugin is typically a combination of HML/CSS/JavaScript and native code used in order to extend the PhoneGap capabilities.

The main advantages you get when using this plugin are that you can keep the SQLite database in a user data location that is known and can be reconfigured, there are no more size limits, and the database can be encrypted using **SQLcipher** (for a complete reference, refer to the online documentation at `http://sqlcipher.net/documentation/`).

From a developer's point of view, there is no change in the API except the prefix; it means that instead of opening a database accessing the `window` object like this:

```
window.openDatabase();
```

You have to refer to the plugin like this:

```
sqlitePlugin.openDatabase();
```

Understanding the Files API

The PhoneGap Files API is an implementation of two different W3C APIs, the Directories and System API and the File API (you can find the complete specifications on the W3C website at `http://www.w3.org/TR/file-system-api/` and `http://www.w3.org/TR/file-upload.`) The PhoneGap Files API is not a complete implementation of the W3C specification; the missing piece is the synchronous filesystem interface implementation. Asynchronous JavaScript APIs are a bit more complex to use because you have to work with multiple nested functions but this should not be a big issue; in fact, it's something web developers are all too familiar with.

 The main difference between asynchronous and synchronous JavaScript execution is that in the first case, you can run several processes simultaneously and avoid "freezing" the user interface. With the introduction of web workers in JavaScript, it's possible to avoid this issue but this is totally beyond the scope for this book; you can find more information about web workers on the Mozilla website at `https://developer.mozilla.org/en-US/docs/DOM/Using_web_workers`.

In order to access the device filesystem, you can use the `requestFileSystem` method of the `LocalFileSystem` object; all the methods of this object are defined in the `window` object. The method accepts the following four arguments:

- The type of storage (temporary or persistent)
- The amount of space in bytes to be allocated on the device storage
- The success handler
- The error handler

When you want to access the device filesystem, the resulting code looks as shown the following snippet:

```
window.requestFileSystem(/*storage*/, /*size*/, onSuccess, onError);
```

For the `storage` argument, you need to specify one of the following two pseudo constants defined in the `LocalFileSystem` object:

- `LocalFileSystem.PERSISTENT`: This indicates that the storage cannot be removed by the user agent without the app's or user's permission.
- `LocalFileSystem.TEMPORARY`: This indicates that the files stored in the requested space can be deleted by the user agent or by the system without the app's or user's permission

The size of the requested sandbox storage is expressed in bytes; for example, in order to make the code more readable, you can use the syntax (4 x 1024 x 1024) to allocate 4 KB instead of the bytes number 4,194,304.

 The device hard disk is not completely open to the app's view. A limited portion of the hard disk is dedicated to a single app alone; this is the app **sandbox**. The idea behind the app sandbox is that each app can only access its own sandbox and some higher-level directories owned by the operating system. The structure of the high-level directories varies depending on the operating system.

The onSuccess handler receives a FileSystem object as an argument. The two properties defined for this object are name and root. Accessing the name property of the object makes it possible to read the name of the filesystem; accessing the root property allows you to get a reference to the root directory of the app sandbox. This is shown here:

```
function onSuccess(fileSystem){

    console.log(fileSystem.name);
    var currentRoot = fileSystem.root;

}
```

The onError handler receives a FileError object as an argument; this object represents different errors using several pseudo constants defined in the object itself, as shown here:

```
function onError(fileError){

    console.log(fileError.code);

}
```

If the location of the file or directory is known, you can use the resolveLocalFileSystemURI method of the LocalFileSystem object to access it. This method accepts the following three arguments:

♦ The URI of the file or directory
♦ The success handler (onSuccess)
♦ The error handler (onError)

If you want to access, for instance, the external storage of an Android device, you can use the following syntax:

```
window.resolveLocalFileSystemURI('file:///mnt/sdcard',
                               onSuccess, onError);.
```

The onSuccess function receives as argument a DirectoryEntry or FileEntry object depending on the kind of path entered (that is, a directory or file); the onError handler receives a FileError object as argument.

The values of the code property are summarized by the following pseudo constants:

- FileError.NOT_FOUND_ERR (returned value 1): This means the file or directory required by the app cannot be found

- FileError.SECURITY_ERR (returned value 2): This means the file or directory is outside the app sandbox or the app does not have the rights to access it

- FileError.ABORT_ERR (returned value 3): This is thrown when the abort method of the reader or writer is called

- FileError.NOT_READABLE_ERR (returned value 4): This means that the file or directory required by the app cannot be read

- FileError.ENCODING_ERR (returned value 5): This means a path or local URI used as an argument in the resolveLocalFileSystemURI method of the LocalFileSystem object is malformed

- FileError.NO_MODIFICATION_ALLOWED_ERR (returned value 6): This means the app attempted to write to a file or directory that cannot be modified due to the actual state of the filesystem

- FileError.INVALID_STATE_ERR (returned value 7): This means the app accesses a file that is used by another process

- FileError.SYNTAX_ERR (returned value 8): This is self-explanatory; this occurs due to the syntax error

- FileError.INVALID_MODIFICATION_ERR (returned value 9): This means the modification requested by the app is invalid; an example of such an error is moving a directory into its own child

- FileError.QUOTA_EXCEEDED_ERR (returned value 10): This means the app requested a storage amount greater than the allowed storage quota

- FileError.TYPE_MISMATCH_ERR (returned value 11): This means the app attempted to access a file or directory but the entry is not of the expected type (that is, a directory is returned instead of a file)

- FileError.PATH_EXISTS_ERR (returned value 12): This means the app failed to create a file or directory due to the existence of a file or directory with the same path

Reading directories and files

Only after getting access to the filesystem is it possible to read the device directories, subdirectories, and content. Again, the `onSuccess` handler used as an argument in the `requestFileSystem` method receives a `FileSystem` object. Through the `root` property of this object, it's possible to access a `DirectoryEntry` object and then create a `DirectoryReader` object able to read all the entries available in the current directory. This is shown here:

```
function onSuccess(fileSystem){

    var currentRoot = fileSystem.root;
    var reader = currentRoot.createReader();

}
```

The `DirectoryReader` object exposes one method named `readEntries`. It can be used in order to read the entries and, due to the asynchronous nature of the File API, it accepts a success and a failure handler. Similar to what's happening for the `resolveLocalFileSystemURI` method, the success handler receives an array of `DirectoryEntry` or `FileEntry` objects according to the kind of item that is listed (that is, a directory or a file).

Time for action – listing folders

Get ready to explore the folders of the device's persistent storage. Use the following steps:

1. Open the command-line tool and create a new project using the Cordova CLI tool you installed before. This will create a new directory called `FileSystem` in your current working directory:

   ```
   $ cordova create FileSystem
   ```

2. Move to the directory you just created:

   ```
   $ cd FileSystem
   ```

3. Add the platforms you want to test on the device API. For this example, we add the Android platform:

   ```
   $ cordova platform add android
   ```

4. Add the File API plugin using the following command:

   ```
   $ cordova plugin add cordova-plugin-file
   ```

5. Go to the www folder, open the index.html file, and add a div element with the id value as fileslist inside the body of the app:

```
<div id="fileslist"></div>
```

6. We will now add a deviceready event listener in the JavaScript section. The onDeviceReady function has to be called once the deviceready event is fired:

```
document.addEventListener("deviceready", onDeviceReady, false);
```

7. In the body of the onDeviceReady function, request access to the device filesystem specifying the success and failure handlers you will define next and request a persistent storage of 0 KB; you need to specify a quota only when writing to the device filesystem:

```
function onDeviceReady() {
    var size = 0;
    window.requestFileSystem(LocalFileSystem.PERSISTENT, size,
      onFileSystemSuccess, onFileSysError);
}
```

8. Define the error handler that will notify you when the code throws an error:

```
function onFileSysError(error){
    alert("Error Code: " + error.code);
}
```

9. Define the success handler and inside its body, create a new DirectoryReader object and use this object to read all the directory contents. We need to pass a new function parseDirectories, which will actually iterate through the list of directories. The directory entries will be passed automatically as an argument to this function:

```
function onFileSystemSuccess(fileSystem){
    var reader = fileSystem.root.createReader();
    reader.readEntries(parseDirectories,onFileSysError);
}
```

10. Define the parseDirectories function and add the following snippet to it:

```
function parseDirectories(entries){
    var str = '<ul>';

    for (var i = 0, len = entries.length; i < len; i++) {
        if (entries[i].isDirectory) {
            str += '<li>' + entries[i].fullPath + '</li>';
        }
    }
```

```
    str += "</ul>";

    document.getElementById("fileslist").innerHTML+= str;

}
```

We read the entries and for each entry in the list, we check whether it's a directory or a file. If it's a directory, we append the directory name to the unordered list and ignore it if it's a file. At the end, we add the generated unordered list (`ul`) to the `div` named `fileslist` we previously created.

When this code runs in an actual device, it will list all the directories in the persistent storage.

The entire source code of this example is provided as follows:

```html
<!DOCTYPE html>

<html>
    <head>
        <!--Other section removed for sake of simplicity -->
        <title>File Example</title>
    </head>

<body>

<div id="fileslist"></div>

<script type="text/javascript" src="cordova.js"></script>

<script type="text/javascript">

document.addEventListener("deviceready", onDeviceReady, false);

function onDeviceReady() {
    var size = 0;
    window.requestFileSystem(LocalFileSystem.PERSISTENT, size,
        onFileSystemSuccess, onFileSysError);
}

function onFileSysError(error){
    alert("Error Code: " + error.code);
}

function onFileSystemSuccess(fileSystem){
    var reader = fileSystem.root.createReader();
    reader.readEntries(parseDirectories,onFileSysError);
}
```

```
function parseDirectories(entries){
    var str = '<ul>';

    for (var i = 0, len = entries.length; i < len; i++) {
        if (entries[i].isDirectory) {
            str += '<li>' + entries[i].fullPath + '</li>';
        }
    }

    str += "</ul>";

    document.getElementById("fileslist").innerHTML+= str;

}

</script>

</body>
</html>
```

What just happened?

The app can now read the list of directories from the device's persistent storage using the asynchronous Files API.

Writing and reading a file's data

To write data to a file, it suffices that the app gets access to the file using the `FileWriter` object. In order to get a `FileWriter` object, you first have to get access to a `DirectoryEntry` object or a `FileEntry` object using the `requestFileSystem` method of the `LocalFileSystem` object.

Once you successfully get access to the filesystem, you can request a file specifying that you want to create it using the `create` flag:

```
Function onFileSystemSuccess(fileSystem){

    var root = fileSystem.root;
    root.getFile('data.txt', {create: true},
                 onGetFile, onGetFileError);

}
```

There are two flags available within the Files API that can be used as arguments of the getFile and getDirectory methods: create and exclusive. The create flag is used to indicate that the file or directory should be created; the exclusive flag takes effect only when the create flag is set to true and it causes the file or directory creation to fail if it already exists.

As with the other Files API, the getFile method is asynchronous and requires a success and failure handler. Once in the success handler, it's possible to create a FileWriter object using the createWriter method of the FileEntry object received as an argument. The createWriter method also requires the success and failure handlers, as shown here:

```
function onGetFile(file){

    file.createWriter(onGetWriter, onGetWriterError);

}
```

Once again, you have two other handlers, which means only after three callback functions, can you write some content into the file you just created:

```
function onGetWriter(writer){

    writer.write('Hello PhoneGap Files API!');

}
```

You can't write binary data from JavaScript in PhoneGap using a FileWriter object; this is a limitation of the framework because it passes data between the native and JavaScript layers as a string. One possible solution is to write a plugin that translates a Base64 string into binary data.

When you perform the write operation, several events occur. For each such event, there is a corresponding property available on the FileWriter object:

- The onwritestart event is called when the FileWriter object starts to write the file; it receives as an argument a ProgressEvent object.

- The onwrite event gets called when the FileWriter object has successfully completed the write operation; it receives as an argument a ProgressEvent object.

- The `Onabort` event is called when the write operation has been interrupted by calling the `abort` method of `FileWriter`; it receives as an argument a `ProgressEvent` object.

- The `Onerror` event is called when the write operation fails; it receives as an argument the `ProgressEvent` object. In order to understand why the error occurs, you can access the `FileError` object stored in the `target.error` property of the event object.

The `FileWriter` object contains other properties as well. For a complete overview, refer to the online guide available at `http://docs.phonegap.com/en/edge/cordova_file_file.md.html#FileWriter`.

Using the `ProgressEvent` object, you can access the bytes loaded, the total bytes, and the nature of the event (that is, `abort`, `writeend`, and so on) using the `loaded`, `total`, and `type` properties:

```
function onGetWriter(writer){

    writer.onwrite = function(evt){

        console.log(evt.loaded, evt.total, evt.type);

    }

    writer.write('Hello PhoneGap Files API!');

}
```

> If you try to call sequentially the `write` method of the `FileWriter` object, only the first string will be added to the file. You have to wait until the `writeend` event is fired in order to write other data to the file.

When you want to read a file, you can use a `FileReader` object. This object works similarly to the `FileWriter` object. When using it, several events occur: the `onabort` and `onerror` properties of the `FileWriter` object act similarly to the `FileReader` ones. The properties related only to the `FileReader` object are as follows:

- `onloadstart`: The function stored in this property is called when the `FileReader` object starts to read a file; it receives a `ProgressEvent` object as an argument.

- `onload`: The function stored in this property is called when the read operation has successfully completed; it receives a `ProgressEvent` object as an argument.

- ◆ `onloadend`: The function stored in this property is called when the read operation is completed (regardless of whether it succeeded or failed); it receives a `ProgressEvent` object as argument.

The `FileReader` object allows you to read the file data in the following four different ways:

- ◆ `readAsDataURL`: This reads the file and returns the content of the specified file as a Base64-encoded data URL

- ◆ `readAsText`: This reads a file and returns the data as a string encoded by default in UTF-8

- ◆ `readAsBinaryString`: This reads the file as binary and returns the data as a binary string

- ◆ `readAsArrayBuffer`: This reads the file and returns the data as `ArrayBuffer`

In order to put into practice what you just learned, you will now see how to parse the device's persistent storage, recover the first available image, and render it in the app's web view.

Here is the complete source code for writing a text file to the phone storage:

```html
<!DOCTYPE html>
<html>
    <head>
        <!--Other section removed for sake of simplicity -->
        <title>File Example</title>
    </head>
<body>
<script type="text/javascript" src="cordova.js"></script>

<script type="text/javascript">

document.addEventListener("deviceready", onDeviceReady, false);

function onDeviceReady() {
    var size = 0;
    window.requestFileSystem(LocalFileSystem.PERSISTENT, size,
        onFileSystemSuccess, onFileSysError);
}

function onFileSystemSuccess(fileSystem){
    var root = fileSystem.root;
```

```
        root.getFile('data.txt', {create: true}, onGetFile,
            onFileSysError);
    }

    function onGetFile(file){
        file.createWriter(onGetWriter, onFileSysError);
    }

    function onGetWriter(writer){

        writer.onwrite = function(evt){
            console.log(evt.loaded, evt.total, evt.type);
        }

        writer.write('Hello PhoneGap Files API!');
    }

    function onFileSysError(error){
        alert("Error Code: " + error.code);
    }

    </script>
    </body>
    </html>
```

Time for action – reading and rendering an image

Get ready to render the first available image in the device's storage into the PhoneGap default app template. Refer to the following steps:

1. Open the command-line tool and create a new PhoneGap project named ReadingFile.

2. Add the File API plugin using the following command line:

   ```
   $ cordova plugin add cordova-plugin-file
   ```

3. Go to the www folder, open the index.html file, and add an img tag with the id value as firstImage inside the main div of the app following the deviceready one:

   ```
   <img id='firstImage' />
   ```

4. Go to the www/js folder, open the index.js file, and define a new function named requestFileSystem:

```
Function requestFileSystem() {
    // The request of access to the file system will go here

}
```

5. Define the error handler in order to get the code of every possible error:

```
Function onError(error){

    alert(error.code);

}
```

6. In the body of the requestFileSystem function, access the device filesystem using the requestFileSystem function of the LocalFileSystem object, define the success and failure handlers, and inside the success handler, access the root filesystem:

```
window.requestFileSystem(LocalFileSystem.PERSISTENT, 0,

                 onFileSystemSuccess, onError);
```

 You are requesting a 0 bytes quota because you are just reading a file; you need to specify a quota only when writing to the device filesystem.

7. Once you get access to the root filesystem, you can create a DirectoryReader object in the success handler and start to explore the root filesystem using the readEntries asynchronous method of the object:

```
var root = fileSystem.root;
var reader = root.createReader();

reader.readEntries(function(entries){

    for (var i = 0, entry; entry = entries[i]; i++){

        // Here The logic to check if the file is an image

    }

}, onError);
```

8. In order to determine whether a file is an image in the `for` loop, you can first check the `isFile` property of the entry and then use a simple regular expression; when the condition is met, you access the file using the `getFile` method of the root `DirectoryEntry` object specifying the success and the failure handlers:

```
if (entry.isFile && (/\.(gif|jpg|jpeg|png)$/i).test(entry.name)){

    root.getFile(entry.name, {create: false},
                onGetFile, onError);
    break;

}
```

9. In the JavaScript section, define the `onGetFile` function, and in its body, access the real file by using the `file` method of the `FileEntry` object. Once you get access to the file, specify the `onload` and `onerror` handlers and read the file using the `readAsDataURL` method in order to assign the result as the `src` attribute of the `img` tag, as shown here:

```
function onGetFile(fileEntry){

    fileEntry.file(function(file){

        var reader = new FileReader();

        reader.onload = function(evt){

            var img = document.querySelector('#firstImage');
            img.src = evt.target.result;

        };

        reader.onerror = function(evt){

            alert(evt.target.error.code, null);

        };

        reader.readAsDataURL(file);

    }, onError);

}
```

Now test the project on a real device. Take a look at the following complete code provided for a quick review:

```html
<!DOCTYPE html>
<html>
    <head>
        <!--Other section removed for sake of simplicity -->
        <title>File Example</title>
    </head>
<body>

<img id="firstImage" />

<script type="text/javascript" src="cordova.js"></script>

<script type="text/javascript">

document.addEventListener("deviceready", onDeviceReady, false);

function onDeviceReady() {
   var size = 0;
   window.requestFileSystem(LocalFileSystem.PERSISTENT, size,
      onFileSystemSuccess, onError);
}

function onFileSystemSuccess(fileSystem){
   var root = fileSystem.root;
   var reader = root.createReader();

   reader.readEntries(function(entries){
      for (var i = 0, entry; entry = entries[i]; i++){
        if (entry.isFile &&
        (/\.(gif|jpg|jpeg|png)$/i).test(entry.name)){
          root.getFile(entry.name, {create: false}, onGetFile,
            onError);
          break;
        }
      }
   }, onError);

}

function onGetFile(fileEntry){

   fileEntry.file(function(file){
      var freader = new FileReader();

      freader.onload = function(evt){
```

```
      var img = document.querySelector('#firstImage');
      img.src = evt.target.result;
    };

    freader.onerror = function(evt){
      alert(evt.target.error.code);
    };

    freader.readAsDataURL(file);
  }, onError);

}

function onError(error){
    alert("Error Code: " + error.code);
}
</script>
</body>
</html>
```

What just happened?

You explored the filesystem of the device and rendered the first image found as a Base64 data stream in your app. Now that you are somewhat familiar with the File API, it's time to learn how to transfer files from and to a device.

Transferring files

The PhoneGap File API also includes the `FileTransfer` object. As the name suggests, this object allows you to develop apps to download and upload files over the Internet. The methods exposed by the `FileTransfer` object are self-explanatory: `upload`, `download`, and `abort`.

The `upload` method accepts several arguments: the path of the file on the device, a URL to receive the file, the success and failure handlers, an option object, and a Boolean to force the method to accept all the security certificates. (I omitted the Boolean in the next snippet because using it for production is not recommended; an app should accept only the protocols it was designed to deal with.)

```
var fileTransfer = new FileTransfer();
fileTransfer.upload(fileURI, URL, onSuccess, onError, options);
```

The `options` argument is a `FileUploadOptions` object. This object allows you to provide additional information using the following properties:

◆ `chunkedMode`: This is a Boolean value that indicates whether the streaming of the HTPP request is performed without internal buffering. (For a more detailed description of the chunked transfer encoding, you can refer to `http://en.wikipedia.org/wiki/Chunked_transfer_encoding`).

◆ `fileKey`: This is a string that indicates the name of the form element under which the file is uploaded to the server; the default value is `file`.

◆ `fileName`: This is a string that represents the name of the uploaded file; the default value is `image.jpg`.

◆ `mimeType`: This is a string representing the MIME type of the file that will be uploaded; by default, the value is `image/jpg`.

◆ `params`: This is an object that represents key-value pairs to be included in the HTTP request header.

The `onSuccess` handler receives a `FileEntry` object as an argument so that you can immediately access information, such as the filename and full path on the device. The `onError` handler receives a `FileTransferError` object; the properties of this object are as follows:

◆ `code`: This is a number that represents one of the four possible error codes stored in the `FileTransferError` pseudo constants (that is, `FILE_NOT_FOUND_ERR`, `INVALID_URL_ERR`, `CONNECTION_ERR`, and `ABORT_ERR`).

◆ `source`: This is a string representing the URI to the source file.

◆ `target`: This is a string representing the URI to the target file.

◆ `http_status`: This is a number representing the HTTP status code.

The `download` method works in a similar way; the only difference is that the first two arguments are switched and are: the URL to download the file and the system URI (that is, the path) in order to store it on the device, respectively; also, the `options` parameter accepts only HTTP headers. This is shown here:

```
var fileTransfer = new FileTransfer();
fileTransfer.download(URL, filePath, onSuccess, onError, options);
```

The `abort` method can be used to stop a download or an upload operation, once the `onError` handler is called, and the value of the `code` property of its argument is the pseudo constant, `FileTransferError.ABORT_ERR`.

Also, when you set up the wrong path of the file to download, the `code` property of the `FileTransferError` object is equal to `FileTransferError.FILE_NOT_FOUND_ERR` (that is, the value 1).

Only the `onprogress` property is defined in the `FileTransfer` object. As the name suggests, this property is used to store a function that is called whenever a chunk of data is transferred from or to the device.

Next, in order to put into practice what you just learned, you will download a file, show the download progress, and add a link to the file once the download is completed.

Time for action – downloading and saving a file

Get ready to download a file and display in the PhoneGap default app template a progress bar and a link to the file. Refer to the following steps:

1. Open the command-line tool and create a new PhoneGap project named `DownloadFile`:

```
$ cordova create DownloadFile
```

2. Change the directory to `DownloadFile`:

```
$ cd DownloadFile
```

3. Add the File and FileTransfer API plugins using the following commands:

```
$ cordova plugin add cordova-plugin-file-transfer
$ cordova plugin add cordova-plugin-file
```

4. Go to the `www` folder, open the `index.html` file, and add a `progress` tag with the `id` value as `progress` inside the main `div` element of the app below the `deviceready` tag; assign 1 to the `value` attribute and 100 to the `max` attribute:

```
<progress id='progress' value='1' max='100'></progress>
```

5. Define a new JavaScript function named `onDeviceReady` and add it to the `deviceready` listener:

```
document.addEventListener("deviceready", onDeviceReady, false);

function onDeviceReady() {
   var size = 0;
   window.requestFileSystem(LocalFileSystem.PERSISTENT,
      size, onFileSystemSuccess, onError);
}
```

6. For the `onFileSystemSuccess` method, once you get access to the filesystem, create a new `FileTransfer` object and call the `download` method specifying the remote URL, the system root URI, and the success and failure handlers:

```
function onFileSystemSuccess(fileSystem){
    var fileTransfer = new FileTransfer();
    var url = 'http://s3.amazonaws.com/mislav/
        Dive+into+HTML5.pdf';

    fileTransfer.download(encodeURI(url),
            fileSystem.root.toURL() + '/' + 'html5.pdf',
            fileDownloaded,
            onError);

    fileTransfer.onprogress = function(evt){

        if (evt.lengthComputable){

            var tot = (evt.loaded / evt.total) * 100;

            var element = document.querySelector('#progress');
            element.value = Math.round(tot);
        }
    }
}
```

7. Define the success and failure event callback functions. For any error, we will alert the entire `error` object as a JSON string, as shown here:

```
function fileDownloaded(entry){
    alert("Success");
}

function onError(error){
    alert(JSON.stringify(error));
}
```

8. Now run your project on a real device. The file will be downloaded and the progress will be shown in the progress bar. Once it's done, you can verify the downloaded file in your device.

The complete source code of this example is provided as follows:

```html
<!DOCTYPE html>
<html>
    <head>
        <!--Other section removed for sake of simplicity -->
        <title>File Example</title>
    </head>
    <body>

<progress id='progress' value='1' max='100'></progress>

<script type="text/javascript" src="cordova.js"></script>

<script type="text/javascript">

    document.addEventListener("deviceready", onDeviceReady, false);

    function onDeviceReady() {
        var size = 0;
        window.requestFileSystem(LocalFileSystem.PERSISTENT, size,
          onFileSystemSuccess, onError);
}

        function onFileSystemSuccess(fileSystem){
            var fileTransfer = new FileTransfer();
            var url = 'http://s3.amazonaws.com/mislav/
              Dive+into+HTML5.pdf';

            fileTransfer.download(encodeURI(url),
                    fileSystem.root.toURL() + '/' + 'html5.pdf',
                      fileDownloaded,
                      onError);

            fileTransfer.onprogress = function(evt){

                if (evt.lengthComputable){

                var tot = (evt.loaded / evt.total) * 100;
```

```
                var element = document.querySelector('#progress');
                element.value = Math.round(tot);
            }
        }
    }

    function fileDownloaded(entry){
        alert("Success");
    }

    function onError(error){
        alert(JSON.stringify(error));
    }

</script>
</body>
</html>
```

What just happened?

You initiated a file download, displayed a progress bar, and rendered a link to the file. You will notice a problem because most platforms don't provide a PDF reader inside the WebView. In short, the user will not be able to read the file, neither in the app nor in the external browser. In order to open a native app to read the file, you have to use an external plugin. You will discover in the next chapter how to integrate a plugin in your app and how to solve this problem.

Summary

In this chapter, you learned how to save data on the device and how to handle the most common limitations. You also learned how the Files API works and looked at its features.

In the next chapter, you will learn how to use the Contact API to work with contacts in the device and Camera API, in order to capture an image using the device camera.

6

Using the Contacts and Camera APIs

In the last chapter, we saw how to get the best out of the Files and Storage plugins. Now that your knowledge of PhoneGap is coming together well, it's time to add some interaction to the device itself. The main goal of this chapter is to help you to understand the usage of the Contacts API of PhoneGap and to interact with the device media using the Camera and Media Capture API.

In this chapter, you will:

- ◆ Get an overview of the PhoneGap Contacts API and its objects and properties
- ◆ Learn how to use the Contacts API to read and filter the contacts stored on the device
- ◆ Understand the difference between the Camera and Capture API
- ◆ Learn how to capture images from the device camera using the Camera API
- ◆ Learn how to handle various media types such as images, audio, and video using the Media Capture API

The Contacts API

You can easily access the contact information stored on a device using the PhoneGap API. The Contacts API is an implementation of the W3C's Pick Contacts Intent API (an intent that enables access to a user's address book service from inside a web application). You can read more about the W3C specifications at `http://www.w3.org/TR/contacts-api/`.

The required functionalities of the Contacts API are provided by the Contacts plugin identified by the name `cordova-plugin-contacts`. This plugin supports major platforms.

For a complete list of all the supported platforms, refer to the documentation at `http://docs.phonegap.com/en/edge/cordova_contacts_contacts.md.html#Contacts`.

In order to start the interaction with the device contacts, you can use the `create` or `find` methods defined in the `contacts` object stored in the `navigator` object:

```
var contact = navigator.contacts.create(properties);
navigator.contacts.find(contactFields, contactSuccess, contactError,
    contactFindOptions);
```

In order to understand how these methods work in a better way, let's explore the most relevant objects that are involved with them: `Contact`, `ContactName`, `ContactField`, `ContactFindOptions`, and `ContactError`.

The ContactName object

The `ContactName` object is used in the PhoneGap framework in order to store all the details of a contact name. The object is stored in the `name` property of the `Contact` object.

The properties of the `ContactName` object are all strings and are self-explanatory:

- `formatted`: This represents the complete name of the contact
- `familyName`: This represents the contact's last name
- `givenName`: This represents the contact's first name
- `middleName`: This represents the contact's middle name
- `honorificPrefix`: This represents the contact's prefix (for example, Mr. or Dr.)
- `honorificSuffix`: This represents the contact's suffix (for example, Esq.)

The ContactField object

The `ContactField` object is a generic object used in the PhoneGap framework in order to represent a field of the `Contact` object. The generic nature of this object makes it reusable across several fields.

The properties of the `ContactField` object are as follows:

- `type`: This is a string that represents the type of field; possible values are home, work, mobile, and so on
- `value`: This is a string representing the value of the field such as a phone number or an e-mail address
- `pref`: This is a Boolean value that indicates whether the user preferred value is returned in a specific field.

When the ContactField object is used in the photos property of the Contact object, the type property represents the type of a returned image (for example, a URL or Base64-encoded string).

The ContactAddress object

The ContactAddress object is the object stored in the addresses property of the Contact object. The addresses property is an array where multiple addresses can be associated with each contact.

The properties of the ContactAddress object are as follows:

- pref: This is a Boolean value that indicates whether the returned ContactAddress object is the preferred value of the user for the ContactAddress object

- type: This is a string that indicates what type of address is stored in the ContactAddress object (for example, home and office)

- formatted: This is a string that represents the complete address that is formatted for display

- streetAddress: This is a string that represents the complete street address

- locality: This is a string that represents the city or locality that is part of the ContactAddress object

- region: This is a string that represents the state or region that is part of the ContactAddress object

- postalCode: This is a string that represents the zip code or postal code associated with the locality stored in the ContactAddress object

- country: This is a string that represents the name of the country stored in the ContactAddress object

There is a limitation in Android 2.x (that is, the pref property is not supported) and several limitations on Android 1.x. Also, iOS does not support the formatted property. Always refer to the online documentation to verify the status of the support for the ContactAddress object.

The ContactOrganization object

The ContactOrganization object represents all the details of a company, organization, and so on, that the stored contact belongs to. The object is stored in the array contained in the organizations property of the Contact object.

The properties of the ContactOrganization object are as follows:

- pref: This is a Boolean value that indicates whether the returned ContactOrganization object is the preferred value of the user for the ContactOrganization object
- type: This is a string that indicates what type of address is stored in the ContactOrganization object (for example, work and other)
- name: This is a string that represents the name of the organization stored in the ContactOrganization object
- department: This is a string that represents the department of the organization who the contact works for
- title: This is a string that represents the contact's title in the organization

The name, department, and title properties are partially supported on iOS; the pref and type properties are badly supported on Android 1.x and Android 2.x.

The Contact object

The Contact object represents all the details of a contact stored in the device database. A Contact object can be saved, removed, and copied from the device contact database using the save, remove, and clone methods defined on the object itself. The save and remove methods accept two arguments in order to handle the success and failure of the save or remove operation:

```
var contact = navigator.contacts.create({'displayName': 'Giorgio'});

contact.save(onContactSaved, onContactSavedError);
contact.remove(onContactRemoved, onContactRemovedError);
```

The error handlers receive the same ContactError object as an argument; the success handlers receive the saved contact or a snapshot of the current database when a contact is successfully removed.

The ContactError object contains the information about the occurred error in the code property. The values that can be returned are as follows:

- ContactError.UNKNOWN_ERROR
- ContactError.INVALID_ARGUMENT_ERROR

- ◆ ContactError.TIMEOUT_ERROR
- ◆ ContactError.PENDING_OPERATION_ERROR
- ◆ ContactError.IO_ERROR
- ◆ ContactError.NOT_SUPPORTED_ERROR
- ◆ ContactError.PERMISSION_DENIED_ERROR

When creating a new Contact object, you can define the contact properties or pass them as an object one by one when calling the create method. The properties of the Contact object are as follows:

- ◆ id: This is a string used as a globally unique identifier
- ◆ displayName: This is a string that represents the name of the Contact object for display to the end users
- ◆ name: This is an object containing all the information of a contact name; the object used to store this information is ContactName
- ◆ nickname: This is a string that represents the casual name of a contact
- ◆ phoneNumbers: This is an array of all the contact's phone numbers; the array items are instances of the ContactField object
- ◆ emails: This is an array of all the contact's e-mail addresses; the array items are instances of the ContactField object
- ◆ addresses: This is an array of all the contact's addresses; the array items are instances of the ContactAddresses object
- ◆ ims: This is an array of all the contact's instant messages accounts; the array items are instances of the ContactField object
- ◆ organizations: This is an array of all the organizations the contact belongs to; the array items are instances of the ContactOrganization object
- ◆ birthday: This is a Date object that represents the birthday of the contact
- ◆ note: This is a string that represents a note about the contact
- ◆ photos: This is an array of all the contact's photos; the array items are instances of the ContactField object
- ◆ categories: This is an array of all the contact's defined categories; the array items are instances of the ContactField object
- ◆ urls: This is an array of all the web pages associated with the contact; the array items are instances of the ContactField object

The Contact object's properties are not fully supported across all platforms. In fact, operating system fragmentation makes it difficult to handle this information consistently.

For instance, the `name`, `nickname`, `birthday`, `photos`, `categories`, and `urls` properties are not supported on Android 1.x. Likewise, the `categories` property is supported neither on Android 2.x. nor iOS.

On iOS, the items returned in the `photos` array contain a URL that points to the app's temporary folder. This means that this content is deleted when the app exits and that you have to handle it if you want the user to find the app in the same status he/she left. The `displayName` property is not supported on iOS and will be returned as null, unless there is `ContactName` defined. If the `ContactName` object is defined, then a composite name or nickname is returned.

Filtering contact data

We have already mentioned the `find` method available in the `navigator.contacts` object. Using this method, an app can find one or multiple contacts in the device's contact database. The `find` method accepts four arguments. The first one is an array that contains the name of the fields of the `Contact` object that have to be returned. The second and third are the success and error handlers. The last one represents the filtering options that you may wish to apply to the current search.

In order to apply a filter to the current search, you can instantiate a new `ContactFindOptions` object and populate the `filter` and `multiple` properties. The `filter` property is a case-insensitive string that will act as a filter on the fields of the `Contact` objects returned by the `find` method. The `multiple` property is `false` by default and is the one to use in order to receive multiple `Contact` objects in the success handler. Try out the following example to understand how these properties work.

Time for action – searching device contacts

We will now see an example of getting all the contacts from the device and listing them down:

1. Create a new project using the PhoneGap CLI:

   ```
   $ phonegap create ContactsApi
   ```

2. Change the current working directory to the directory that is newly created:

   ```
   $ cd ContactsApi
   ```

3. Add the required platforms to the project. We will add Android for this example:

   ```
   $ phonegap platform add android
   ```

4. Install the Contacts plugin to the project:

   ```
   $ phonegap plugin add cordova-plugin-contacts
   ```

5. In the `www/index.html` file, you need to replace the content and add the following code. To start with, let's create an event listener and bind that to a function. In the following code, when the device is ready, the `OnDeviceReady` method will be fired:

```
<script type="text/javascript" charset="utf-8">
    document.addEventListener("deviceready", onDeviceReady,
        false);
</script>
```

6. Now, let's add the content for the `OnDeviceReady` method:

```
function onDeviceReady() {
    var options = new ContactFindOptions();
    options.filter = "";
    options.multiple=true;
    var fields = ["displayName", "name", "addresses"];
    navigator.contacts.find(fields, onSuccess, onError,
        options);
}
```

With the preceding code, you are creating a new `ContactFindOptions` object and setting filters/properties to the object. Based on the filter that you set, the function will return all the matching contacts. In this example, we have given an empty filter, which means we get back all the contacts from the device.

If you want to limit the search only to a particular name, you can provide the filter as shown here:

```
options.filter = "John";
```

You can also restrict the list of fields that the function is going to return. If you feel that it's enough to have only a few fields for output, you can mention them in the list of fields. For example, we have restricted the output to only the display name, `name` object, and address of the contacts.

7. When the function is executed successfully, it will return the values to the `OnSuccess` event and will trigger the `OnError` event when there are some issues. So let's define the `OnSuccess` and `OnError` events to define what we are going to do with the output:

```
function onSuccess(contacts) {
    for (var i = 0; i < contacts.length; i++) {
        console.log("Display Name = " + contacts[i].
            displayName);
    }
};

function onError(contactError) {
    alert('onError!');
};
```

8. When we have acquired all of the contacts, we loop through the `contacts` object and display the name of the contact in the console.

The following complete code has been given for your reference. When you test the code in an actual device, you can see the contact names in the console:

```
<script type="text/javascript" charset="utf-8">
document.addEventListener("deviceready", onDeviceReady, false);

function onDeviceReady() {
    var options = new ContactFindOptions();
    options.filter = "";
    options.multiple=true;
    var fields = ["displayName", "name", "addresses"];
    navigator.contacts.find(fields, onSuccess, onError, options);
}

function onSuccess(contacts) {
    for (var i = 0; i < contacts.length; i++) {
        console.log("Display Name = " + contacts[i].displayName);
    }
};

function onError(contactError) {
    alert('onError!');
};
</script>
```

What just happened?

You filtered the contact database based on the options defined by the `ContactFindOptions` object and you refined the result using the API provided by the PhoneGap framework.

Time for action – adding a new contact

We will directly go to the example of creating a new contact entry using the Contacts API. The code for this is as follows:

```
<script type="text/javascript" charset="utf-8">
    // Binding to the events
    document.addEventListener("deviceready", onDeviceReady, false);
```

```
    // device APIs are ready and available to use
    function onDeviceReady() {
        var myContact = navigator.contacts.create({"displayName":
          "Purus Test"});

        var phoneNumbers = [];

        phoneNumbers[0] = new ContactField('work', '1234567890',
          false);
        phoneNumbers[1] = new ContactField('mobile', '2345678901',
          true); // preferred
        phoneNumbers[2] = new ContactField('home', '3456789012',
          false);

        // You can add any other values of Contact object with name
          and phone numbers
        myContact.phoneNumbers = phoneNumbers;

        myContact.save(onSaveContactSuccess,onSaveContactError);

    }

    function onSaveContactSuccess(contact) {
        alert('saved successfully');
    };

    function onSaveContactError(error) {
        alert(error.code);
    };

</script>
```

The last parameter of `ContactField` expects a Boolean value to denote whether the field is a preferred one. In the preceding example, the second phone number with the value of `true` is set as the preferred number.

What just happened?

We have seen how we can create a new `Contact` object and save this to the device using the Contacts API.

Camera API or Capture API?

The PhoneGap framework implements two different APIs to access media on a device: the Camera API and the Capture API. The main difference between these APIs is that the Camera API can access only the default device camera application, whereas the Capture API can also record audio or video using the default audio and video recording application. Another important difference is that the Capture API allows multiple captures with a single API call.

 The Capture API is an implementation of an abandoned W3C standards draft. As you can see, there are several similarities between the draft and the actual PhoneGap implementation.

Accessing the camera using the Camera API

The Camera API provides access to the device's camera application using the Camera plugin identified by the `cordova-plugin-camera` key. With this plugin installed, an app can take a picture or gain access to a media file stored in the photo library and albums that the user created on the device. The Camera API exposes the following two methods defined in the `navigator.camera` object:

◆ `getPicture`: This opens the default camera application or allows the user to browse the media library, depending on the options specified in the `configuration` object that the method accepts as an argument

◆ `cleanup`: This cleans up any intermediate photo file available in the temporary storage location (supported only on iOS)

As arguments, the `getPicture` method accepts a success handler, failure handler, and optionally an object used to specify several camera options through its properties as follows:

◆ `quality`: This is a number between `0` and `100` used to specify the quality of the saved image.

◆ `destinationType`: This is a number used to define the format of the value returned in the success handler. The possible values are stored in the following `Camera.DestinationType` pseudo constants:

❑ `DATA_URL(0)`: This indicates that the `getPicture` method will return the image as a Base64-encoded string

❑ `FILE_URI(1)`: This indicates that the method will return the file URI

❑ `NATIVE_URI(2)`: This indicates that the method will return a platform-dependent file URI (for example, `assets-library://` on iOS or `content://` on Android)

- `sourceType`: This is a number used to specify where the `getPicture` method can access an Image. The following possible values are stored in the `Camera.PictureSourceType` pseudo constants: `PHOTOLIBRARY (0)`, `CAMERA (1)`, and `SAVEDPHOTOALBUM (2)`:
  - `PHOTOLIBRARY`: This indicates that the method will get an image from the device's library
  - `CAMERA`: This indicates that the method will grab a picture from the camera
  - `SAVEDPHOTOALBUM`: This indicates that the user will be prompted to select an album before picking an image

- `allowEdit`: This is a Boolean value (the value is `true` by default) used to indicate that the user can make small edits to the image before confirming the selection; it works only in iOS.

- `encodingType`: This is a number used to specify the encoding of the returned file. The possible values are stored in the `Camera.EncodingType` pseudo constants: `JPEG (0)` and `PNG (1)`.

- `targetWidth` and `targetHeight`: These are the width and height in pixels, to which you want the captured image to be scaled; it's possible to specify only one of the two options. When both are specified, the image will be scaled to the value that results in the smallest aspect ratio (the aspect ratio of an image describes the proportional relationship between its width and height).

- `mediaType`: This is a number used to specify what kind of media files have to be returned when the `getPicture` method is called using the `Camera.PictureSourceType.PHOTOLIBRARY` or `Camera.PictureSourceType.SAVEDPHOTOALBUM` pseudo constants as `sourceType`; the possible values are stored in the `Camera.MediaType` object as pseudo constants and are `PICTURE (0)`, `VIDEO (1)`, and `ALLMEDIA (2)`.

- `correctOrientation`: This is a Boolean value that forces the device camera to correct the device orientation during the capture.

- `cameraDirection`: This is a number used to specify which device camera has to be used during the capture. The values are stored in the `Camera.Direction` object as pseudo constants and are `BACK (0)` and `FRONT (1)`.

- `popoverOptions`: This is an object supported on iOS to specify the anchor element location and arrow direction of the popover used on iPad when selecting images from the library or album.

- `saveToPhotoAlbum`: This is a Boolean value (the value is `false` by default) used in order to save the captured image in the device's default photo album.

The success handler receives an argument that contains the URI to the file or data stored in the file's Base64-encoded string, depending on the value stored in the `encodingType` property of the `options` object. The failure handler receives a string containing the device's native code error message as an argument.

Similarly, the `cleanup` method accepts a success handler and a failure handler. The only difference between the two is that the success handler doesn't receive any argument. The `cleanup` method is supported only on iOS and can be used when the `sourceType` property value is `Camera.PictureSourceType.CAMERA` and the `destinationType` property value is `Camera.DestinationType.FILE_URI`.

In order to put into practice what you have learned about the Camera API, let's create an app that can take a picture from the device's default camera application.

Time for action – accessing the device camera

Get ready to access the device's camera and show the user the captured picture. Refer to the following steps:

1. Open the command-line tool and create a new PhoneGap project named `camera`:

   ```
   $ cordova create camera
   ```

2. Change to the directory that is created:

   ```
   $ cd camera
   ```

3. Using the command-line tool, add the Android and iOS platforms to the project:

   ```
   $ cordova platforms add android
   $ cordova platforms add ios
   ```

4. Add the Camera API plugin using the following command line:

   ```
   $ cordova plugin add cordova-plugin-camera
   ```

5. Go to the www folder, open the `index.html` file, and replace the contents with the following code; this code is self-explanatory:

   ```html
   <!DOCTYPE html>
   <html>
     <head>
       <script type="text/javascript" charset="utf-8"
         src="cordova.js"></script>
       <script type="text/javascript" charset="utf-8">

       // Wait for device API libraries to load
   ```

```
document.addEventListener("deviceready",
  onDeviceReady,false);

// device APIs are available
function onDeviceReady() {
}

function getCameraImage() {
  // Take picture using camera and get image source as
    base64-encoded string
  navigator.camera.getPicture(onCaptureSuccess, onError, {
    quality: 20, allowEdit: false, destinationType:
    navigator.camera.DestinationType.DATA_URL });
}

// Called when a photo is successfully retrieved
function onCaptureSuccess(imageData) {
  var smallImage = document.getElementById('cameraImage');
  smallImage.src = "data:image/jpeg;base64," + imageData;
}

// Capture any failures
function onError(message) {
  alert('Error: ' + message);
}
</script>
</head>
<body>
  <button onclick="getCameraImage();">Capture Photo</button>
    <br>
  <img style="display:none;width:60px;height:60px;" id=
    "cameraImage" src="" />
</body>
</html>
```

When the user clicks on the **Capture Photo** button, the getCameraImage()
function will be triggered which in turn uses the navigator.camera.
getPicture() method to capture the image from the device camera and
passes the image data to the onCaptureSuccess() method if the capture is
successful. Later, the data source in encoded string format is assigned to the
<img> tag's source.

6. If you want to enable photo editing capabilities, set the `allowEdit` property to `true` as shown here:

```
navigator.camera.getPicture(onCaptureSuccess, onError, {
    quality: 20, allowEdit: true, destinationType:
    navigator.camera.DestinationType.DATA_URL });
```

7. Once you have made the changes, you need to build the project to try the application on your actual device. To do so, open the command-line tool and launch the `prepare` command, and then the `compile` command from the root of the project:

```
$ cordova prepare
```

```
$ cordova compile
```

> The `prepare` and `compile` commands can be executed from any folder of the project. The `build` command is a shorthand for the `prepare` and `compile` commands.

8. Run the project on your device for each target platform (unfortunately, emulators don't support the camera). To test the app in the actual device platform, you can use the `run` command as shown here:

```
$ cordova run android
```

> Before running this, you need to make your device ready to test, and the steps vary for each platform. For example, you need to enable the USB debugging option on your Android device. For more information on the setup of each platform, you can visit `https://cordova.apache.org/docs/en/edge/index.html`.

As explained in the previous sections, the `cleanup` method works only in iOS. This means that your app should look and work differently depending on the target platform.

When creating a new project with the Cordova command-line tool, a folder named `merges` is created in the root of the project. This folder contains a separate folder for each platform you add to the project; the root folder of a PhoneGap project looks as follows:

```
├── config.xml
├── hooks
├── merges
├── platforms
├── plugins
```

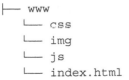

```
├── www
    └── css
    └── img
    └── js
    └── index.html
```

When you have to handle different user interface elements or business logic for a specific target platform, you can place the files you want to merge in the merges/TARGET_PLATFORM folder. You can create the index.html and index.js files, specifically targeted for the iOS platform by implementing the cleanup method.

What just happened?

You accessed the device camera and learned how to handle different implementations of the Camera API on Android and iOS using the merge feature of Cordova. Once you have built the app, if you go to the platform-specific folders (platforms/android/assets/www and platforms/ios/www) and open the index.js file, you will see that they differ from each other.

Controlling the camera popover

The getPicture method in iOS (and specifically on iPad) returns a CameraPopoverHandle object when the sourceType property value is one of the following pseudo constants defined in the Camera.PictureSourceType object: SAVEDPHOTOALBUM or PHOTOLIBRARY. Using this object, it's possible to control the position of the popover dialog box created when the getPicture method is called.

The CameraPopoverHandle object exposes only the setPosition method that requires a CameraPopoverOptions object as an argument. This object allows you to specify the coordinates, dimensions, and position of the arrow of this dialog box:

```
var popoverOptions = new CameraPopoverOptions();
popoverOptions.x = 220;
popoverOptions.y = 600;
popoverOptions.width = 320;
popoverOptions.height = 480;
popoverOptions.arrowDir = Camera.PopoverArrowDirection.ARROW_DOWN;
```

You can reach the same result with a more compact syntax, specifying the properties in the constructor of the CameraPopoverOptions object:

```
var popoverOptions = new CameraPopoverOptions(220, 600, 320, 480,
  Camera.PopoverArrowDirection.ARROW_DOWN);
```

It's also possible to specify coordinates, position, and arrow direction, using the `popoverOptions` property of the `cameraOptions` object:

```
cameraOptions.popoverOptions = {
            x : 220,
            y :  600,
            width : 320,
            height : 480,
            arrowDir : Camera.PopoverArrowDirection.ARROW_DOWN

};
```

The pseudo constants defined in the `PopoverArrowDirection` object match the native iOS constants defined in the `UIPopoverArrowDirection` class:

```
Camera.PopoverArrowDirection = {
                             ARROW_UP: 1,
                             ARROW_DOWN: 2,
                             ARROW_LEFT: 4,
                             ARROW_RIGHT: 8,
                             ARROW_ANY: 15
};
```

This option is extremely useful when you want to have control over the position of the dialog box when the orientation of the device changes. In the next example, you will control the position and size of the dialog box in order to override the default behavior.

If you want to use different iOS devices (for example, an iPhone 5 and 4S to test different screen sizes) for development, you have to create a provisioning file and add it to the device. You can either create one provisioning file for all your projects, or you can use one file for each project. In order to create a new file for your device, you have to do the following:

1. Read the device ID by clicking on the serial number you get on the first screen you get in iTunes when connecting the device.

2. Go to the Apple developer portal, log in, and add a new development device to your account.

3. Create and download a new provisioning file (you should already have a certificate available, otherwise read the information available in the Apple developer portal at `https://developer.apple.com/support/technical/certificates/`).

4. Add the provisioning file to your device using the Xcode Organizer window (in Xcode, navigate to **Window | Organizer**).

It's also now possible to just plug in your device and let Xcode register and manage the provisioning profiles for you.

Time for action – controlling the position of the camera roll

Use the following steps to change the position of the default camera roll dialog box on an iPad:

1. Go to the `merges/ios/js` folder of the PhoneGap project you previously created, open the `index.js` file, and add a new function named `initAdditionalOptions`:

```
initAdditionalOptions: function(){

    // Additional options will be defined here

}
```

2. In the body of the `initAdditionalOptions` function, specify the device photo album as the source of the `getCamera` method as well as the size and position of the popover dialog box:

```
app.cameraOptions.sourceType = Camera.PictureSourceType.
                               SAVEDPHOTOALBUM;

app.cameraOptions.popoverOptions = new CameraPopoverOptions(220,
600, 320, 480, Camera.PopoverArrowDirection.ARROW_DOWN);
```

3. Add a call to the `initAdditionalOptions` function at the end of the `deviceready` event handler:

```
deviceready: function() {
    // All the events handling initializations are here
    app.initAdditionalOptions();

}
```

4. Open the command-line tool and run the `prepare` and `compile` commands (or the `build` command) in order to test the project on a real device.

What just happened?

You handled the size and position of a default dialog box on iOS on an iPad using only JavaScript.

The Media Capture API

Modern devices offer a huge range of media capabilities to the user; at present, people can record a video, record some audio, and take a picture, and use all of these media in their communication flow.

The Media Capture API works asynchronously as most of the PhoneGap APIs and provides access to the audio, image, and video capture capabilities of the device. In order to start working with this API, you have to install the plugin to your project as shown here:

```
$ phonegap plugin add cordova-plugin-media-capture
```

Once done, you can access the `capture` object stored in the `navigator.device` object:

```
var capture = navigator.device.capture;
```

Once you get access to the `capture` object, it's possible to detect which video, audio, and image formats are supported by the device through the following properties:

- `supportedAudioModes`
- `supportedImageModes`
- `supportedVideoModes`

Each property returns an array of the `ConfigurationData` objects; each item of the array represents a supported media type. There are three properties defined in the `ConfigurationData` object that you can use to clearly identify the media types supported by the device:

- `type`: This is a lower case string that represents the supported media type following the RFC2046 standard explained at `http://www.ietf.org/rfc/rfc2046.txt` (that is, `video/3gpp`, `video/quicktime`, `image/jpeg`, `audio/amr`, and so on)
- `height`: This is a number that represents the height of the supported image or video in pixels (the property returns `0` when the object represents a supported audio format)
- `width`: This is a number that represents the width of the supported image or video in pixels (the property returns `0` when the object represents a supported audio format)

> At the time of writing, the `ConfigurationData` object is not implemented in any supported platform. In fact, each of the arrays stored into the `supportedAudioModes`, `supportedImageModes`, and `supportedVideoModes` properties are empty.

The `capture` object exposes three methods in order to access the video, audio, and image capture capabilities of the device:

◆ `captureVideo`

◆ `captureAudio`

◆ `captureImage`

These methods have the same syntax: each one accepts a success handler, a failure handler, and an `option` object as arguments. The success handler is invoked upon a successful media capture operation and it receives an array of `MediaFile` objects describing each captured file as an argument. The error handler is invoked if an error occurs during a media capture operation or when the user cancels the operation and receives a `CaptureError` object as an argument. The following example captures an image using the device camera:

```
var capture = navigator.device.capture;

capture.captureImage(function(files){

                    console.log(files);

        }, function(error){

            console.log(error);

        });
```

The `MediaFile` object stored in the files array returned by the success handler describes the captured media. The properties of the `MediaFile` object are as follows:

◆ `fullPath`: This is a string that represents the file path on the device including the filename.

◆ `lastModifiedDate`: This is the modification date of the file expressed as the number of milliseconds since January 1, 1970 (refer to `https://developer.mozilla.org/en/docs/JavaScript/Reference/Global_Objects/Date` for more information on the `Date` object in JavaScript).

◆ `name`: This is a string that represents the name of the file. The name is composed by the `lastModificationDate` value and the file extension.

◆ `size`: This is a number that represents the size of the file in bytes.

◆ `type`: This is a string that represents the mime type of the captured file (for example, `image/jpeg`).

The CaptureError object returned to the error handler only has one property, code. This property contains an integer equal to one of the following pseudo constants defined in the CaptureError object:

◆ CaptureError.CAPTURE_INTERNAL_ERR (returned value 0): This means the device failed to capture a video, an image, or sound

◆ CaptureError.CAPTURE_APPLICATION_BUSY (returned value 1): This means the capture application is currently serving another capture request

◆ CaptureError.CAPTURE_INVALID_ARGUMENT (returned value 2): This means the app is using invalid arguments when invoking the API (for example, the limit parameter has a value of less than 1)

◆ CaptureError.CAPTURE_NO_MEDIA_FILES (returned value 3): This means the user exited the camera application or the audio capture application before capturing anything

◆ CaptureError.CAPTURE_NOT_SUPPORTED (returned value 20): This means the requested capture operation is not supported

The option object varies for each method. In fact, the Capture API defines a different object for each kind of capture: CaptureVideoOptions, CaptureAudioOptions, and CaptureImageOptions. All of these objects have the same properties, limits, and modes in common; the duration property is defined only in the CaptureVideoOptions and CaptureAudioOptions objects. The default value of the limit property is 1 and it's used to specify the number of captures the user can do before returning to the app. The duration property is the maximum length of a capture in seconds. The mode property represents the selected video or audio mode.

Support for the configuration options is very fragmented. For instance, the limit property of the CaptureImageOptions and CaptureVideoOptions objects is not supported in iOS. Refer to the documentation at http://docs.phonegap.com/en/edge/cordova_media_capture_capture.md.html#Capture to check the actual status of the implementation.

The most efficient way to manipulate an image is through native code; however, you can also perform simple image manipulations via JavaScript. In order to avoid overcomplicating the following example, we have used HTML Canvas to render an image with some effects.

The <canvas> tag of HTML is a container used to draw graphics on the fly using scripting languages such as JavaScript. It has several inbuilt functions and we are going to use them here.

For more information on HTML5 Canvas, refer to
`http://www.html5canvastutorials.com/`.

Time for action – manipulating images with a canvas

Get ready to apply a sepia effect to an image acquired using the Media Capture API. Execute the following steps:

1. Open the command-line tool and create a new PhoneGap project named `ImageEffect`:

   ```
   $ cordova create ImageEffect
   ```

2. Change the path to the newly created project:

   ```
   $ cd ImageEffect
   ```

3. Add the Media Capture API plugin using the following command:

   ```
   $ cordova plugin add cordova-plugin-media-capture
   ```

4. Add a `canvas` tag with the `id` value as `#manipulatedImage` to the existing markup, in order to use it to render the manipulated image:

   ```
   <canvas id='manipulatedImage' />
   ```

5. Once the `deviceready` event has been fired, access the device camera, which allows the user to access only one image:

   ```
   var capture = navigator.device.capture;
   capture.captureImage(onGetImage, onImageError, {limit: 1});
   ```

6. Define the success handler and access the file information stored in the array that is returned as an argument:

   ```
   function onGetImage(files){

       var currentFile = files[0];

       // Canvas access logic will go here
   }
   ```

7. Get access to the canvas and store a reference to the `2d` context of the canvas, in order to be able to draw content on it:

   ```
   var canvas = document.querySelector('#manipulatedImage');
   var context = canvas.getContext('2d');

   // Image object definition and load will go here
   ```

8. Create an `image` object, assign a handler to the `onload` property, and define the `src` property of the object using the `fullPath` property of the `MediaFile` object:

```
var image = new Image();

image.onload = function(evt) {
    // The image manipulation logic will go here
};

image.src = currentFile.fullPath;
```

9. In the function stored in the `onload` property, draw the image on the canvas, get the pixels, manipulate them, and reassign the pixels to the canvas:

```
var width = canvas.width;
var height = canvas.height;

context.drawImage(this, 0, 0, width, height);

var imgPixels = context.getImageData(0, 0, width, height);
context.putImageData(grayscale(imgPixels), 0, 0, 0, 0, width,
    height);
```

The complete code of this example is provided here for your understanding:

```
<!DOCTYPE html>
<html>
    <head>
        <!--Other section removed for sake of simplicity -->
        <title>Media Capture Example</title>
    </head>
<body>
<canvas id='manipulatedImage' />

<script type="text/javascript" src="cordova.js"></script>

<script type="text/javascript">

    document.addEventListener("deviceready", onDeviceReady, false);

    function onDeviceReady() {
        var capture = navigator.device.capture;
        capture.captureImage(onGetImage, onError, {limit: 1});
        }

    function onGetImage(files){
```

```
       var currentFile = files[0];

       var canvas = document.querySelector('#manipulatedImage');
       var context = canvas.getContext('2d');
       var image = new Image();

       image.onload = function(evt) {
          var width = canvas.width;
          var height = canvas.height;

          context.drawImage(this, 0, 0, width, height);
          var imgPixels = context.getImageData(0, 0, width, height);
          context.putImageData(grayscale(imgPixels), 0, 0, 0, 0,
            width, height);
       };
       image.src = currentFile.fullPath;
   }

   function onError(error){
      alert(JSON.stringify(error));
   }
</script>
</body>
</html>
```

You can find the `grayscale` function and several image effects at
`http://www.html5rocks.com/en/tutorials/canvas/imagefilters/`.

When you refer to any plugins or PhoneGap-specific objects such as
`CameraPopoverOptions`, you have to wait until the `deviceready` event
is fired so that the required objects are available for use:

```
if (typeof window.plugins.CameraPopoverOptions !==
  'undefined'){
    // plugin object is available to be used
}
```

Some plugins define global objects and they can be used to verify that the plugin
is loaded and available to use:

```
function onDeviceReady() {
    console.log(navigator.device.capture);
}
```

Summary

In this chapter, you learned about the Contacts API, how to find contacts from a device, how to filter contacts, and how to save new contacts to a device. You also learned the differences between the Camera and Media Capture APIs and how to use them in your application.

In the next chapter, you will learn how to access the Device Sensor API in order to determine the device orientation, position, and also how to implement the Locations API.

7

Accessing the Device Sensors and Locations API

The use of device sensors opens the doors to sophisticated apps, which may improve user experience and enhance the capabilities of a modern app. It's very important for a mobile developer to understand the power and limitations of device sensors in order to effectively use the APIs provided by the PhoneGap framework. Location data allows a mobile developer to tag every piece of information with the device's position. In this chapter, you will also learn to couple the Location API with your app.

In this chapter, you will:

♦ Learn which are the most common device sensors and how to use them in order to enhance the user experience

♦ Get an overview of the device orientation and device motion events using the accelerometer

♦ Learn how to work with device sensors directly with JavaScript

♦ Learn how to use the Compass API of PhoneGap

♦ Learn about geolocation and how its data is available in the device

♦ Learn how to use the PhoneGap Geolocation API and how to integrate the Google Maps API in an app

Location data allows a mobile developer to tag every piece of information with the device's position. This kind of meat tagging enables the use of very contextualized apps. The PhoneGap framework provides a Geolocation API that is simple to use, easy to understand, and very powerful.

Introducing device sensors

Humans have senses (touch, hear, smell, and so on); a phone has digital "senses": touch, geolocation, orientation, and motion. A sensor is a device component that measures a physical quantity and converts it into a signal that is understandable to software. Modern mobile phones come with a variety of sensors that can support users when completing their daily tasks. By tapping into a device sensor, you can enhance the end user experience and develop sophisticated apps.

Sensors can be hardware-based or software-based. Hardware-based sensors are physical components built into a handset or tablet device. They derive their data by directly measuring specific environmental properties such as acceleration, geomagnetic field strength, or angular change. Software-based sensors are not physical devices, although they mimic hardware-based sensors.

Typical device sensors are the **accelerometer**, **gyroscope**, **compass**, **barometer**, **orientation sensor**, and so on.

Not all devices, nor their operating systems support the same sensors, so you have to know which devices you want to target before considering which sensors to use in your app. The device sensors typically are divided into the following categories:

- Motion sensors
- Environmental sensors
- Position sensors

The **motion sensors** measure acceleration forces and rotational forces along the three axes. Hardware parts such as the accelerometer, gravity sensors, gyroscopes, and rotational vector sensors belong to this category. The **environmental sensors** measure various environmental parameters such as ambient air temperature and pressure, illumination, and humidity. The barometers, photometers, and thermometers belong to this category of sensors. The **position sensors** measure the physical position of a device.

As already mentioned, each operating system offers different sensors. From a developer's point of view, this means that to work on different platforms, you have to understand how sensors work on each one. When working with PhoneGap, you can safely use the **Accelerometer** and **Compass** APIs across different platforms. Furthermore, you can rely on the **onboard browser** capabilities to get additional sensor information such as the device orientation.

The accelerometer is actually made up of three accelerometers and each one measures the changes in velocity (that is, linear acceleration) overtime along the linear path on the axes *x*, *y*, and *z*. Combining the data of the three accelerometers, you can get the device movement and orientation.

The gyroscope is always part of the motion sensors and it measures the rate of rotation around the three axes, usually **roll**, **pitch**, and **yaw**.

The magnetometer measures the strength of the magnetic field surrounding the device and in the absence of any strong local fields, these measurements will refer to the magnetic field of the Earth. In this way, the device is able to determine its **heading** with respect to the geomagnetic North Pole; using the heading values, it's possible to determine the yaw of the device too. Magnetic heading updates are available even if the user has switched off location updates in the settings application; the reported values are positive numbers from **0** to **360**. The real heading of the user, when they are holding the device in landscape mode, is the reported heading plus 90 degrees.

The iOS platform provides all the common sensors a developer can expect such as accelerometer, magnetometer, gyroscope, and the proximity sensor.

The Android platform provides four additional sensors that allows you to monitor various environmental properties: ambient **humidity, luminance**, ambient **pressure**, and ambient **temperature**. All the sensors are hardware-based and are available only if a manufacturer has built them into a device.

 You can find a complete demo of the Android sensors on the Google Play store; just search and install the *Android Sensor Box* app.

The Windows Phone 7.5/8 platform offers wide support for sensors. You can use the **Inclinometer** sensor to detect the pitch, roll, and yaw of the device or you can create complex 3D apps using the **Quaternion** sensor (quaternion is the quotient of two directed lines in a three-dimensional space). For a complete overview of the Windows Phone sensor APIs, please refer to the online documentation at `http://msdn.microsoft.com/ library/windows/apps/windows.devices.sensors`.

The location capabilities of a device rely on several sensors called position sensors. Devices normally use multiple positioning methods to provide different granularities of location data. The sources of position data vary in terms of accuracy, startup time, and power signature, and include the following:

- GPS
- A-GPS
- Cell tower triangulation
- Wi-Fi triangulation
- IP address

With the continuous evolution of sensors, end user expectations are growing and the quality of the apps available on the market is increasing.

> **Lapka Electronics** released a set of sensors and an app that is able to translate environmental data to read values easily. Using their sensors and app, you can measure electromagnetic pollution, humidity, amounts of nitrates in raw foods and drinking water, and so on. More information about these sensors is available online at http://mylapka.com/.

Sensors and human-computer interaction

Sensors evolved and are still evolving very fast and are influencing how creative people are designing apps. The new generation of apps rely on voice commands, gestures, and more in order to allow the user to control apps in a more intuitive way. An app is now able to perceive the user's intentions based on the sensor data it collects. The use of sensors to make apps (and computers) more intuitive to control is known as **perceptual computing**. This initiative is led by Intel and has various applications including video conferencing, gaming, and so on.

By contrast, **augmented reality** is about extending how humans interface with the physical world through computers. Using an augmented reality interface, you can add additional information to the external environment and create amazing and useful apps. On mobile devices, the implementation of an augmented reality application heavily depends on the sensors on the devices, such as video cameras and orientation sensor.

A nice example of the kind of interactions you can reach through sensors is an app for iOS named **Car Finder**. The app stores the position of a car when the user takes a picture of it and then provides to the user the information needed to find where he/she had parked the car.

The capability to use sensors and the data they return is increasingly paramount for mobile developers. The sensors supported by PhoneGap are limited, but PhoneGap is simply a wrapper that makes it easier to separate your presentation layer from the native device code. For this reason, you can start to write additional native code around the PhoneGap wrapper to extend its capabilities.

> An interesting resource on sensor development is available on the Microsoft website at http://research.microsoft.com/en-us/groups/ sendev/, where you can find papers and resources to help you get started with sensors.

Accelerometer

The PhoneGap Accelerometer API allows you to detect the device movement change values relative to device orientation. Note that the accelerometer detects the values as a delta movement relative to the current device position. Even more important, it takes into consideration the effect of gravity (that is, *9.81 m/s²*), so that when a device is lying flat on a table facing up, the value returned should be *x = 0, y = 0*, and *z = 9.81*.

As with any other plugin, you have to install the plugin before you can use it in your project. The plugin can be added to your project using the following command:

```
$ cordova plugin add cordova-plugin-device-motion
```

Once the plugin is installed on the project, a `navigator.Accelerometer` global object, is created and it is available to use once the `deviceready` event is fired. However, it is recommended that you still check for its presence before using it:

```
document.addEventListener("deviceready", onDeviceReady, false);

function onDeviceReady() {
    if( typeof navigator.accelerometer === "undefined"){
        //plugin is ready now
    }
}
```

You can detect the device acceleration data using the `getCurrentAcceleration` method or by setting up a watcher through the `watchAcceleration` method. Both methods are available on the `navigator.accelerometer` object and accept similar arguments.

The `getCurrentAcceleration` method accepts a success and a failure callback function as an argument and doesn't return anything. The `watchAcceleration` method accepts an additional argument in order to define the options and return a reference to the current watcher.

In order to constantly watch the acceleration data, you have to define the frequency at which you want to recover data and store the value returned by the `watchAcceleration` method in a variable:

```
var options = {frequency: 300};
var currentAcceleration = navigator.accelerator.watchAcceleration
                        (onSuccess, onFailure, options);
```

The `onSuccess` handler receives an `Acceleration` object as an argument, accessing its property and making it possible to read the acceleration on each axis:

```
function onSuccess(acceleration) {

    console.log('Acceleration X: ' + acceleration.x );
    console.log('Acceleration Y: ' + acceleration.y);
    console.log('Acceleration Z: ' + acceleration.z );

};
```

The failure handler doesn't receive any argument, but it's pretty useful to handle possible errors when accessing the device's accelerometer:

```
function onError() {

    console.log('Error accessing the accelerometer');

};
```

In order to stop watching the accelerometer data, it's sufficient to call the `clearWatch` method defined on the `accelerator` object, passing the reference to the variable previously used to store the result of the `watchAcceleration` method:

```
navigator.accelerometer.clearWatch(currentAcceleration);
```

This method doesn't accept any additional handler.

 All the sensor APIs of PhoneGap work in a similar way; you will always have to use a `getCurrentSENSOR` and a `watchSENSOR` method (where `SENSOR` is the name of the sensor) to obtain data from the sensor. In order to stop watching a sensor, you will always use the `clearWatch` method.

Detecting shakes

Using the information recovered from the accelerometer API, it's possible to understand whether the user is shaking the device.

Device orientation events

The cordova-plugin-device-motion plugin only supports access to the acceleration information. In order to handle the orientation changes, you have to rely on the JavaScript APIs of the target platform browser. When you want to update the user interface when the device orientation changes, you have to use CSS media queries; any other business logic can be handled using JavaScript due to the fact that PhoneGap uses the web view to render the app user interface.

Using JavaScript, you can set up a listener for the `orientationchange` event and another listener for the `deviceorientation` event in order to handle the device orientation. The first event is fired each time the orientation of the device changes; the second event is fired when the physical orientation of the device changes. Both the listeners have to be registered to the `window` object:

```
window.addEventListener('orientationchange', EVENT_HANDLER);
window.addEventListener('deviceorientation', EVENT_HANDLER);
```

The `orientationchange` event handler is commonly used to detect the screen orientation after it has changed. Once the orientation changes, the app receives a notification for several events. The following table summarizes these events and the orientation property value:

Device and user gesture	Events fired	Orientation
iPad to landscape	resize	0
	orientationchange	90
iPad to portrait	resize	90
	orientationchange	0
iPhone to landscape	resize	0
	orientationchange	90
iPhone to portrait	resize	90
	orientationchange	0
Android phone to landscape	orientationchange	90
	resize	90
Android phone to portrait	orientationchange	0
	resize	0

The deviceorientation event is very powerful. It returns to the handler an instance of the DeviceOrientationEvent event with the following information:

- alpha: This returns the rotation of the device around the *z* axis
- beta: This returns the rotation of the device around the *x* axis
- gamma: This returns the rotation of the device around the *y* axis

> In order to improve the performance of your app, consider using the event-handler function to do no more than save current values from the sensor data into variables. Then, move your calculations or DOM manipulations into a new function executed at a fixed time.

Handling orientation with JavaScript

It's time to put into practice what you have learned about the device orientation events. Let's work on a very basic sample that is able to show the screen orientation in a div element rotated according to the device's physical orientation.

Time for action – handling device orientation with JavaScript

Execute the following steps:

1. Open the command-line tool and create a new PhoneGap project named orientationevents, and add the platforms you want to target for this example.

2. Install the plugin to your project:

   ```
   $ phonegap plugin add cordova-plugin-device-motion
   ```

3. Go to the www folder, open the index.html file, and add div with the #orientation ID inside the main div of the app beneath #deviceready:

   ```html
   <div class="app">
       <h1>Apache Cordova</h1>
       <div id="deviceready">
           ......
       </div>
       <div id="orientation">
       </div>
   </div>
   ```

4. Go to the css folder and define two new rules inside the index.css file to give a border and a bigger font size to div and its content. You can even add the CSS styles directly to the head section of your HTML page:

```
#orientation{

    width: 230px;
    border: 1px solid rgb(10, 1, 1);

}

#orientation p{
    font-size: 36px;
    font-weight: bold;
    text-align: center;

}
```

5. Go to the js folder, open the index.js file, and define a new function to easily detect whether the device can handle the orientationchange and deviceorientation events. Alternatively, you can even have the script embedded in your HTML page:

```
orientationSupported: function(){

    try {
        return 'DeviceOrientationEvent' in window &&
        window['DeviceOrientationEvent'] !== null;
    } catch (e) {
        return false;
    }

}
```

6. In the deviceready function, add two listeners if the device supports the orientationchange and deviceorientation events:

```
if(orientationSupported){

    window.addEventListener('orientationchange',
                            orientationChanged);
    window.addEventListener('deviceorientation',
                            updateOrientation);
```

```
}else{

    alert('Orientation not supported!');

}
```

7. Define the `orientationChanged` event handler and use it to print the current device orientation on screen:

```
orientationChanged: function(){

    var element = document.querySelector('#orientation');
    element.innerHTML = '<p>' + window.orientation + '</p>';

}
```

8. Define the handler for the `deviceorientation` event and use the information provided by the device's sensor to change the 3D transformation of the `div` orientation:

```
updateOrientation: function(event){

    var alpha = event.alpha,
    beta = event.beta,
    gamma = event.gamma;

    var element = document.querySelector('#orientation');
    var rotation = 'rotateZ(' + alpha + 'deg) rotate
        (' + beta + 'deg) rotateY(' + gamma + 'deg)';
// For brevity the browser prefixes have been removed
        element.style.transform = rotation;

}
```

9. Open the command-line tool again, locate the main project folder, and then compile the app and test it on every platform you previously added.

Here is the complete code of this example:

```
<!DOCTYPE html>
<html>
    <head>
        <!--Other section removed for sake of simplicity -->
        <title>Media Capture Example</title>
        <style>
```

```
      #orientation{
        width: 230px;
        border: 1px solid rgb(10, 1, 1);
      }

      #orientation p{
        font-size: 36px;
        font-weight: bold;
        text-align: center;
      }
    </style>
</head>
<body>
  <div class="app">
    <h1>Apache Cordova</h1>
    <div id="deviceready"></div>
    <div id="orientation"></div>
  </div>

  <script type="text/javascript" src="cordova.js"></script>
  <script type="text/javascript">

    document.addEventListener("deviceready", onDeviceReady,
      false);

    function onDeviceReady() {
      if(orientationSupported){
        window.addEventListener('orientationchange',
          orientationChanged);
        window.addEventListener('deviceorientation',
          updateOrientation);
      }else{
        alert('Orientation not supported!');
      }
    }

    orientationSupported: function(){
      try {
        return 'DeviceOrientationEvent' in window &&
        window['DeviceOrientationEvent'] !== null;
      } catch (e) {
        return false;
      }
    }
```

```
orientationChanged: function(){
  var element = document.querySelector('#orientation');
  element.innerHTML = '<p>' + window.orientation + '</p>';
}

updateOrientation: function(event){

  var alpha = event.alpha,
  var beta = event.beta,
  var gamma = event.gamma;

  var element = document.querySelector('#orientation');
  var rotation = 'rotateZ(' + alpha + 'deg) rotate(' + beta +
    'deg) rotateY(' + gamma + 'deg)';
  // For brevity the browser prefixes have been removed
  element.style.transform = rotation;
}

    </script>
  </body>
</html>
```

What just happened?

You handled the orientation events using JavaScript and deployed the result to a device using PhoneGap. The app is able to get the device screen orientation and the current position in real time.

Compass

The PhoneGap Compass API allows you to obtain the direction that the device is pointing to. The compass is a sensor that detects the direction or heading in which the device is pointed and returns the heading of the device in degrees using values from 0 to 359.99. The Compass API works similarly to the Accelerometer API; in fact, you can read the current device heading or you can define a watcher in order to continuously read the heading value.

The Compass API is available on the compass property of the navigator object and exposes the following functions:

- ◆ compass.getCurrentHeading: This reads the current compass heading through a handler

- ◆ compass.watchHeading: This reads the compass heading at a specific time interval through a handler and returns a reference to it

- ◆ compass.clearWatch: This stops a previously defined time interval reading handler

The getCurrentHeading and watchHeading functions accept very similar arguments; the only difference is the last argument of the watchHeading function that allows you to configure it. In order to read the current heading of the device, it is sufficient to execute the getCurrentHeading function, specifying a success and an error handler:

```
navigator.compass.getCurrentHeading(onSuccess, onError);
```

The onSuccess handler receives as an argument a CompassHeading object with the following properties:

- ◆ magneticHeading: This is the heading in degrees from 0 to 359.99

- ◆ trueHeading: This is the heading relative to the geographic North Pole in degrees

- ◆ headingAccuracy: This is the deviation between the reported heading and the true heading in degrees

- ◆ timestamp: This is the time at which this heading was determined

The error handler receives a CompassError object as an argument; the CompassError object has a property named code that returns two possible values such as CompassError. COMPASS_INTERNAL_ERR or CompassError.COMPASS_NOT_SUPPORTED:

```
function onError (error) {
    switch(true){

        case error.code == CompassError.COMPASS_INTERNAL_ERR:
        navigator.notification.alert('Compass Error!', null, 'Info',
          'OK');
        break;

        case error.code == CompassError.COMPASS_NOT_SUPPORTED:
        navigator.notification.alert('Compass Unavailable!', null,
          'Info', 'OK');
        break;

        default:
        navigator.notification.alert('Generic Error!', null,'Info',
          'OK');

    }
}
```

The watchHeading function works like the getCurrentHeading function. The only difference is that it accepts an additional CompassOption object that allows you to set up how often to retrieve the compass heading in milliseconds (that is, frequency) and the change in degrees required to initiate the success handler (that is, filter):

```
var options = {frequency: 300};
var currentHeading = navigator.compass.watchHeading(
                    onSuccess, onError, options);
```

In order to stop watching the heading value changes, it is sufficient to use the clearWatch function and the reference to the current heading watcher:

```
clearWatch(currentHeading);
```

The trueHeading property of the CompassHeading object is not supported on Android. It returns the same value as magneticHeading, and the headingAccuracy value will always be 0 as there is no difference between magneticHeading and trueHeading.

On iOS, the trueHeading property is returned only when location services are running using the watchLocation function.

Creating a compass

Reading the current heading of a device is a common task for a developer in several use cases such as traffic apps, augmented reality apps, or any app that incorporates a sense of direction. Let's see how to create a complete compass with PhoneGap:

The images used to render the compass are available under the Creative Commons license at http://commons.wikimedia.org/wiki/File:Compass.svg. Before starting to work on this example, download the image and create three separate PNG files for the background, dial, and arrow. As it's a SVG vector file, you can handle each layer of the image and edit it as your wish. To edit the image, you can use any vector editing applications such as Adobe Illustrator or a free application such as Inkscape.

Time for action – using the Compass API

Execute the following steps:

1. Open the command-line tool, create a new PhoneGap project named `compass`, and add the platforms you want to target for this example.

2. Add the Compass API plugin using the following command:

   ```
   $ cordova plugin add cordova-plugin-device-orientation
   ```

3. Go to the www folder and open the `index.html` file. The three `div` tags are used to handle the compass arrows and the background:

   ```
   <section id="compass">
       <div id="compassbg"></div>
       <div id="north"></div>
       <div id="arrow"></div>
   </section>
   ```

4. Go to the `css` folder, open the `index.css` file, and define the rules needed to have a separate background for each element of the compass:

   ```
   #compassbg {
       background-image: url(../img/Compass.png);
   }
   #north {
       background-image: url(../img/arrow_direction.png);
   }

   #arrow {
       background-image: url(../img/arrow_beta.png);
   }

   #compass, #arrow, #north, #compassbg {
       background-repeat: no-repeat;
       background-size: cover;
       position: fixed;
       width: 286px;
       height: 286px;

   }
   ```

5. Go to the `js` folder, open the `index.js` file, and add a new variable in order to store a reference to the watcher that you will define to monitor the device heading. Alternatively, you can have the scripts embedded directly in the page:

```
var currentHeading = null;
```

6. Locate the `deviceready` function and add inside it the snippet of code needed in order to check the device heading every 150 milliseconds:

```
var options = {frequency: 150};
currentHeading = navigator.compass.watchHeading
    (onCompassSuccess,onCompassError, options);
```

7. Create a new function named `onCompassSuccess` and inside its body, start to read the heading data stored in the received argument; use it to rotate the compass elements:

```
function onCompassSuccess(heading){
    var magneticHeading = heading.magneticHeading;
    var trueHeading = heading.trueHeading;

    var compass = document.querySelector('#compassbg');
    var north = document.querySelector('#north');

    var compassRotation = 'rotate(' + magneticHeading + 'deg)';
    var northRotation = 'rotate(' + trueHeading + 'deg)';
    var compassSytle = compass.style;
    var northStyle = north.style;

    compassStyle.transform = compassRotation;
    northStyle.transform = northRotation;
}
```

8. Define the function to capture the failures, if any:

```
function onCompassError(error){
    alert("Error with Compass");
}
```

9. Open the command-line tool again, locate the main project folder, compile the app, and test it on every platform you previously added.

For the example, we just saw, you can find the complete code here:

```
<!DOCTYPE html>
<html>
    <head>
```

```html
<!--Other section removed for sake of simplicity -->
<title>Media Capture Example</title>
<style>
  #compassbg {
    background-image: url(../img/Compass.png);
  }
  #north {
    background-image: url(../img/arrow_direction.png);
  }

  #arrow {
    background-image: url(../img/arrow_beta.png);
  }

  #compass, #arrow, #north, #compassbg {
    background-repeat: no-repeat;
    background-size: cover;
    position: fixed;
    width: 286px;
    height: 286px;
  }

</style>

</head>
<body>

  <section id="compass">
    <div id="compassbg"></div>
    <div id="north"></div>
    <div id="arrow"></div>
  </section>

  <script type="text/javascript" src="cordova.js"></script>

  <script type="text/javascript">
    var currentHeading = null;

    document.addEventListener("deviceready", onDeviceReady,
      false);

    function onDeviceReady() {
```

```
        var options = {frequency: 150};

        currentHeading = navigator.compass.
          watchHeadingonCompassSuccess,onCompassError, options);
      }

    function onCompassSuccess(heading){
      var magneticHeading = heading.magneticHeading;
      var trueHeading = heading.trueHeading;

      var compass = document.querySelector('#compassbg');
      var north = document.querySelector('#north');

      var compassRotation = 'rotate(' + magneticHeading + 'deg)';
      var northRotation = 'rotate(' + trueHeading + 'deg)';
      var compassSytle = compass.style;
      var northStyle = north.style;

      compassStyle.transform = compassRotation;
      northStyle.transform = northRotation;
    }

    function onCompassError(error){
      alert("Error with Compass");
    }
    </script>
  </body>
</html>
```

What just happened?

You implemented a real, cross-platform compass using the PhoneGap API. In the process, you learned how to use a pretty complex feature of mobile device sensors.

An introduction to geolocation

The term **geolocation** is used in order to refer to the identification process of the real-world geographic location of an object. Devices that are able to detect the user's position are becoming more common each day and we are now used to getting content based on our location (**geo targeting**).

Using the **Global Positioning System (GPS)**—a space-based satellite navigation system that provides location and time information consistently across the globe—you can now get the accurate location of a device. During the early 1970s, the US military created Navstar, which is a defense navigation satellite system. Navstar was the system that created the basis for the GPS infrastructure used today by billions of devices. As of October 2014, 68 GPS satellites have been successfully placed in the orbit around the Earth (refer to `http://en.wikipedia.org/wiki/List_of_GPS_satellite_launches` for a detailed report about the past and planned launches).

The location of a device is represented through a point. This point is comprised of two components: latitude and longitude. There are many methods for modern devices to determine the location information; these include the following:

- GPS
- IP address
- GSM/CDMA cell IDs
- Wi-Fi and Bluetooth MAC address

Each approach delivers the same information; what changes is the accuracy of the device's position. The GPS satellites continuously transmit information that can parse; for example, the general health of the GPS array, roughly where all of the satellites are in orbit, information on the precise orbit or path of the transmitting satellite, and the time of the transmission. The receiver calculates its own position by timing the signals sent by any of the satellites in the array that is visible.

> The process of measuring the distance from a point to a group of satellites in order to locate a position is known as **trilateration**. The distance is determined using the speed of light as a constant, along with the time that the signal left the satellites.

The emerging trend in mobile development is GPS-based "people discovery" apps such as Highlight, Sonar, Banjo, and Foursquare. Each app has different features and has been built for different purposes, but all of them share the same killer feature: using location as a piece of metadata in order to filter information according to the user's needs.

The PhoneGap Geolocation API

The Geolocation API is not a part of the HTML5 specification, but it is tightly integrated with mobile development. The PhoneGap Geolocation API and the W3C Geolocation API mirror each other; both define the same methods and relative arguments. There are several devices that already implement the W3C Geolocation API; for those devices, you can use native support instead of the PhoneGap API.

As per the HTML specification, the user has to explicitly allow the website or the app to use the device's current position.

The Geolocation API is exposed through the `geolocation` object child of the `navigator` object and consists of the following three methods:

- `getCurrentPosition()`: This returns the device position
- `watchPosition()`: This watches for changes in the device position
- `clearWatch()`: This stops the watcher for the device's position changes

The `watchPosition()` and `clearWatch()` methods work in the same way that the `setInterval()` and `clearInterval()` methods work; in fact, the first one returns an identifier that is passed in to the second one. The `getCurrentPosition()` and `watchPosition()` methods mirror each other and take the same arguments: a success and a failure callback function and an optional `configuration` object. The `configuration` object is used in order to specify the maximum age of a cached value of the device's position, in order to set a timeout after which the method will fail and specify whether the application requires only accurate results:

```
var options = {maximumAge: 3000, timeout: 5000,
                enableHighAccuracy: true };
navigator.geolocation.watchPosition(onSuccess, onFailure, options);
```

 Only the first argument is mandatory, but it's recommended to always handle the failure use case.

The success handler function receives a `Position` object as an argument. Accessing its properties, you can read the device's coordinates and the creation timestamp of the object that stores the coordinates:

```
function onSuccess(position) {

    console.log('Coordinates: ' + position.coords);
    console.log('Timestamp: ' + position.timestamp);

}
```

The `coords` property of the `Position` object contains a `Coordinates` object; so far, the most important properties of this object are `longitude` and `latitude`. Using those properties, it's possible to start to integrate positioning information as relevant metadata in your app.

The failure handler receives a `PositionError` object as an argument. Using the `code` and the `message` property of this object, you can gracefully handle every possible error:

```
function onError(error) {
    console.log('message: ' + error.message);
    console.log ('code: ' + error.code);

}
```

The `message` property returns a detailed description of the error and the `code` property returns an integer; the possible values are represented through the following pseudo constants:

◆ `PositionError.PERMISSION_DENIED`: This indicates that the user denied the app to use the device's current position

◆ `PositionError.POSITION_UNAVAILABLE`: This indicates that the position of the device cannot be determined

 If you want to recover the last available position when the POSITION_ UNAVAILABLE error is returned, you have to write a custom plugin that uses the platform-specific API. Android and iOS have this feature. You can find a detailed example at `http://stackoverflow. com/questions/10897081/retrieving-last-known- geolocation-phonegap`.

◆ `PositionError.TIMEOUT`: This indicates that the specified timeout has elapsed before the implementation could successfully acquire a new `Position` object.

 JavaScript doesn't support constants such as Java and other object-oriented programming languages. With the term "pseudo constants," I refer to those values that should never change in a JavaScript app.

One of the most common tasks to perform with the device position information is to show the device location on a map. You can quickly perform this task by integrating Google Maps in your app; the only requirement is a valid API key. To get the key, use the following steps:

1. Visit the APIs' console at `https://code.google.com/apis/console` and log in with your Google account.
2. Select **APIs & auth** in the left-hand side menu.
3. Select **Google Maps JavaScript API** and activate the service.

Time for action – showing device position with Google Maps

Get ready to add a map renderer to the PhoneGap default app template. Execute the following steps:

1. Open the command-line tool and create a new PhoneGap project named `MapSample`:

   ```
   $ cordova create MapSample
   ```

2. Change the working directory to the newly created project:

   ```
   $ cd MapSample
   ```

3. Add the required platform to the project. For example, we will add Android to this project:

   ```
   $ cordova platform add android
   ```

4. Add the Geolocation API plugin using the following command:

   ```
   $ cordova plugin add cordova-plugin-geolocation
   ```

5. Go to the www folder, open the `index.html` file, remove all the existing content, and add a `div` element with the `id` value as `#map` inside the `body` tag:

   ```
   <div id='map'></div>
   ```

6. Include the `cordova.js` file that will be added to the app at runtime:

   ```
   <script type="text/javascript" src="cordova.js"></script>
   ```

7. Add a new `script` tag to include the Google Maps JavaScript library. Replace the `YOUR_API_KEY` value with your actual Google Maps API key:

   ```
   <script type="text/javascript"
       src="https://maps.googleapis.com/maps/api/js?key=
         YOUR_API_KEY&sensor=true">
   </script>
   ```

8. Create a new CSS style to give an appropriate size to the `div` element and its content:

   ```
   #map{

       width: 280px;
       height: 230px;
       display: block;
       margin: 5px auto;
       position: relative;

   }
   ```

9. In the JavaScript section, define a new function named `initMap`:

```
function initMap(lat, long){

    // The code needed to show the map and the
    // device position will be added here

}
```

10. In the body of the function, define an `options` object in order to specify how the map has to be rendered:

```
var options = {

    zoom: 8,
    center: new google.maps.LatLng(lat, long),
    mapTypeId: google.maps.MapTypeId.ROADMAP

};
```

11. Add to the body of the `initMap` function the code to initialize the rendering of the map and to show a marker representing the current device's position over it:

```
var map = new google.maps.Map(document.getElementById('map'),
options);

var markerPoint = new google.maps.LatLng(lat, long);

var marker = new google.maps.Marker({

    position: markerPoint,
    map: map,
    title: 'Device\'s Location'

});
```

12. Define a function to use as the success handler and call from its body the `initMap` function previously defined:

```
function onSuccess(position){

    var coords = position.coords;
    initMap(coords.latitude, coords.longitude);

}
```

13. Define another function in order to have a failure handler that is able to notify the user that something went wrong:

```
function onFailure(error){

    alert(error.message);

}
```

14. Go into the `deviceready` function and add as the last statement the call to the Geolocation API needed to recover the device's position:

```
navigator.geolocation.getCurrentPosition(app.onSuccess,
    app.onFailure, {timeout: 5000, enableAccuracy: false});
```

15. Open the command-line tool, build the app, and then run it on your testing devices:

```
$ cordova build
$ cordova run android
```

Here is the project's complete code for your reference:

```html
<!DOCTYPE html>
<html>
<head>
<title>GeoLocation Example</title>

<style>
  #map{
    width: 280px;
    height: 230px;
    display: block;
    margin: 5px auto;
    position: relative;
  }
</style>

</head>
<body>

<div id='map'></div>

<script type="text/javascript" src="cordova.js"></script>
```

```html
<script type="text/javascript" src="https://maps.googleapis.com/maps/
  api/js?key=YOUR_API_KEY&sensor=true"></script>

<script type="text/javascript">
  var currentHeading = null;

  document.addEventListener("deviceready", onDeviceReady, false);

  function onDeviceReady() {
    navigator.geolocation.getCurrentPosition(onSuccess, onFailure,
      {timeout: 5000, enableAccuracy: false});
  }

  function onSuccess(position){
    var coords = position.coords;
    initMap(coords.latitude, coords.longitude);
  }

  function initMap(lat, long){
    var options = {
      zoom: 8,
      center: new google.maps.LatLng(lat, long),
      mapTypeId: google.maps.MapTypeId.ROADMAP
    };

    var map = new google.maps.Map(document.getElementById('map'),
      options);

    var markerPoint = new google.maps.LatLng(lat, long);

    var marker = new google.maps.Marker({
      position: markerPoint,
      map: map,
      title: 'Device\'s Location'
    });
  }

  function onFailure(error){
    alert(error.message);
  }

</script>
</body>
</html>
```

What just happened?

You integrated Google Maps inside an app. This map is an interactive map most users are familiar with—the most common gestures are already working and the Google Street View controls are already enabled.

> To successfully load the Google Maps API on iOS, it's mandatory to whitelist the `googleapis.com` and `gstatic.com` domains. Open the `.plist` file of the project as source code (right-click on the file and then **Open As | Source Code**) and add the following array of domains:
>
> ```
> <key>ExternalHosts</key>
> <array>
>     <string>*.googleapis.com</string>
>     <string>*.gstatic.com</string>
> </array>
> ```

Other geolocation data

In the previous example, you only used the `latitude` and `longitude` properties of the `position` object that you received. There are other attributes that can be accessed as properties of the `Coordinates` object:

- `altitude`: This gives the height of the device, in meters, above the sea level
- `accuracy`: This gives the accuracy level of the latitude and longitude, in meters; it can be used to show a radius of accuracy when mapping the device's position
- `altitudeAccuracy`: This gives the accuracy of the altitude in meters
- `heading`: This gives the direction of the device in degrees clockwise from true north
- `speed`: This gives the current ground speed of the device in meters per second

The `latitude` and `longitude` properties are the best supported of these properties, and the ones that will be most useful when communicating with remote APIs. The other properties are mainly useful if you're developing an application for which geolocation is a core component of its standard functionality, such as apps that make use of this data to create a flow of information contextualized to the geolocation data. The `accuracy` property is the most important of these additional features, because as an application developer, you typically won't know which particular sensor is giving you the location and you can use the `accuracy` property as a range in your queries to external services.

There are several APIs that allow you to discover interesting data related to a place; among these, the most interesting are the Google Places API and the Foursquare API.

The Google Places and Foursquare online documentation is very well organized and it's the right place to start if you want to dig deeper into these topics. You can access the Google Places docs at `https://developers.google.com/maps/documentation/javascript/places` and Foursquare at `https://developer.foursquare.com/`.

Summary

In this chapter, you learned how to work with device sensors to enhance the functionality of your app. You also learned how to get the geolocation information from a device and how to integrate external geolocation service in the app. Furthermore, you continued to gain an understanding of the PhoneGap APIs that allow you to create powerful native apps.

In the next chapter, you will start to work with some advanced concepts of using PhoneGap.

8
Advanced PhoneGap

Enter globalization and localization if you want your application to reach users of multiple countries and cultures. Your application should be able to support multiple languages/locales and this can be achieved by using the Globalization API and libraries related to localization. Think of support for multiple gestures if you want the application to be more advanced and user-friendly.

In this chapter, you will:

- Learn how to use the Globalization API to support the locale of the mobile app user
- Learn how to localize the application by showing the content in multiple languages based on the user's choice
- Get an overview of the libraries providing gesture support
- Learn how to implement multiple touch gestures to enhance the user experience
- Learn how to remove the 300 ms delay introduced during click events

Using the Globalization API

In computing, globalization, internationalization, and localization are means of adapting computer software to different languages, regional differences, and the technical requirements of a target market. Let's see these in detail.

The term **localization** refers to all the activities needed before your app can be deployed in different languages and according to local cultural conventions. Before starting to localize an app, you have to **internationalize** your code by removing any language and cultural dependencies and design your code in order for it to be adapted to various languages without engineering changes. You can then localize your app, translate client-facing content and labels, and otherwise adapt it so that it works well in a particular locale.

The term **locale** refers to a collection of settings or preferences to be used in localization. A locale is often described as a language and country pair such as en-US, de-AT, it-IT, and so on.

The term **globalization** stands for the combination of internationalization and localization.

There are some odd-looking abbreviations in which a number is used to indicate the number of letters between the first and last letters used to refer to internationalization, localization, and globalization:

- `i18n`: This stands for internationalization
- `l10n`: This stands for localization
- `g11n`: This stands for globalization

> Software internationalization is a huge topic because it covers plurals, dates, special characters, and so on. Discussing all of them is beyond the scope of this book. If you are interested in learning more about internationalization, take a look at the GNU project gettext (`http://www.gnu.org/software/gettext/manual/`), the globalize project (`https://github.com/jquery/globalize`), or the Jed project (`http://slexaxton.github.io/Jed/`).

PhoneGap offers great support for localization through the Globalization API that is accessible through the `globalization` object. You can install the plugin to your project as shown here:

```
$ cordova plugin add cordova-plugin-globalization
```

The `globalization` object is a child of the `navigator` object, and therefore has global scope. In order to access the `globalization` object, it's enough to type the following line of code:

```
var globalization = navigator.globalization;
```

The `globalization` object exposes several asynchronous methods that have a similar signature. In fact, usually most methods accept an argument, a success and a failure handler, and optionally an `options` object:

```
globalization.methodName(argument, onSuccess, onError, options);
```

Not all the methods accept an argument and the `options` object; some of them accept only a success and a failure handler. The failure handler receives a `GlobalizationError` object as an argument. There are two properties defined on this object: `message` and `code`. The first one contains a string describing the error details; the second one contains an integer equal to one of the following pseudo constants defined in the `GlobalizationError` object:

♦ `GlobalizationError.UNKNOWN_ERROR` (return value 0): This means a generic error occurred

♦ `GlobalizationError.FORMATTING_ERROR` (return value 1): This means an error occurred during a formatting operation

♦ `GlobalizationError.PARSING_ERROR` (return value 2): This means an error occurred during a parsing operation

♦ `GlobalizationError.PATTERN_ERROR` (return value 3): This means an error occurred while recovering a currency, date, or number pattern

The Globalization API exposes the following methods defined in the `navigator.globalization` object:

♦ `getPreferredLanguage`: This returns the string identifier for the device's current language; the string is stored in the `value` property of the object received as an argument in the success handler (for example, `{value: 'English'}`)

♦ `getLocaleName`: This returns the locale identifier according to the device's current language; the string is stored in the `value` property of the object received as an argument in the success handler (for example, `{value: 'en'}`)

♦ `dateToString`: This returns a date formatted as a string according to the client's locale and time zone; the method accepts a `Date` object as the first argument and an optional `options` object as the last argument:

```
var globalization = navigator.globalization;

var today = new Date();
globalization.dateToString(today, onSuccess, onError);
```

The returned result is stored in the `value` property of the object received as an argument in the success handler (for example, `{value: '06/14/2013 12:49 PM'}`).

♦ `stringToDate`: This parses a date formatted as a string, and depending on the device's preferences and calendar, returns the corresponding `Date` object as an argument in the success handler.

- `getDatePattern`: This returns an object received as an argument in the success handler containing the following:

    - A pattern string to format and parse dates according to the device's preferences

    - The time zone of the device

    - The difference in seconds between the device's time zone and the universal time and the offset in seconds between the device's non-daylight saving time zone

    - The client's daylight saving time zone (for example, {pattern: 'dd/MM/yyyy HH:mm', timezone: 'CEST', utc_offset: 3600, dst_offset: 3600})

    This method accepts an optional `options` object through which it's possible to specify the format length (that is, `short`, `medium`, `long`, or `full`) and the data to be returned (that is, `date`, `time`, or `date and time`)

- `getDateNames`: This returns an array of names of the months or days of the week, depending on the device's settings; the array is stored in the `value` property of the object received as an argument in the success handler (that is, {value: Array[12]})

- `isDayLightSavingsTime`: This returns a Boolean stating whether daylight saving time is in effect for a given `Date` object passed as the first argument using the device's time zone and calendar; the value is stored in the `dst` property of the object received as an argument in the success handler (for example, {dst: true})

- `getFirstDayOfWeek`: This returns the first day of the week as a number, depending on the device's user preferences and calendar, assuming that the days of the week are numbered starting from 1 (= Sunday); the string is stored in the `value` property of the object received as an argument in the success handler (for example, {value: 1})

- `numberToString`: This returns the number passed as the first argument formatted as a string according to the client's locale and preferences; the number is stored in the `value` property of the object received as an argument in the success handler (for example, {value: '12,456,246'})

- `stringToNumber`: This returns the string passed as the first argument formatted as a number according to the client's locale and preferences; the number is stored in the `value` property of the object received as an argument in the success handler (for example, {value: 1250.04})

- ◆ `getNumberPattern`: This returns an object received as an argument in the success handler containing the following:

  - ❑ A pattern string to format and parse numbers according to the device's preferences

  - ❑ The number of fractional digits to use when parsing and formatting numbers, the rounding increment to use when parsing and formatting, and so on (for example, `{decimal: '.', fraction: 0, grouping: ',', negative: '-', pattern: '#,##0.###', positive: '', rounding: 0, symbol: '.'}`)

- ◆ `getCurrencyPattern`: This returns an object received as an argument in the success handler containing a pattern string to format and parse currencies according to the currency code passed as the first argument, the device's preferences, the number of fractional digits to use when parsing and formatting numbers, the rounding increment to use when parsing and formatting, the ISO 4217 currency code for the pattern, and so on (for example, `{code: 'EUR', decimal: '.', fraction: 2, grouping: ',', pattern: '$#,##0.00;(¤#,##0.00)', rounding: 0}`)

> Both the `numberToString` and `stringToNumber` methods accept an optional `options` object; through the `type` property of this object, you can specify the format of the number (for example, `decimal`, `percent`, or `currency`).

Through the combination of the data provided by the methods of the `globalization` object, it's possible to handle very complex scenarios and provide a highly localized app to the end user. The Globalization API is a very powerful tool that allows you to work in conjunction with other JavaScript libraries.

Localizing your app

From a development perspective, the common practice is to place the text in resource strings that are loaded at the execution time depending on the user settings. There are several techniques you can use to globalize your app such as storing the translations in **portable object** (**PO**) files, creating a JSON object containing all of them, or loading the localization files dynamically when the app starts. The goal is to deploy an app that is able to select the relevant language resource file at runtime and to handle culture-aware number and date parsing and formatting, plurals, currencies, special characters, validation, and so on.

In the following example, we will learn how to load different language strings in the application using a simple JavaScript library.

Time for action – rendering localized messages

Refer to the following steps to render different messages in your app according to the device's language settings:

1. Open the command-line tool and create a new PhoneGap project called `Globalization`:

```
$ cordova create Globalization
```

2. Add the Globalization API plugin using the following command:

```
$ cordova plugin add cordova-plugin-globalization
```

3. Using the command-line tool, add the platform you want to use for this test (Android, Blackberry, iOS, or Windows Phone 8):

```
$ cordova platforms add android
```

4. Download and save the `l10n.js` file available at `https://github.com/marcelklehr/html10n.js` in the `www/js` folder.

5. Go to the `www` folder and create the JSON file named `langs.json` to store all the required language strings as shown here. A JSON file format is a simple way of storing data like XML. The file will have the same literals repeated for each language:

```
{
  "en": {
    "welcome": "Welcome",
    "english": "English",
    "french": "French",
    "alert": "It's me!"
  },
  "fr": {
    "welcome": "Bienvenu",
    "english": "Anglais",
    "french": "Français",
    "alert": "C'est moi!"
  }
}
```

6. In the `www` directory, edit the `index.html` file and add the following code line in the `head` section to load the JavaScript file to work with multiple languages:

```
<script type="text/javascript" src="js/l10n.js"></script>
```

7. Load the `langs.json` file with the appropriate type as shown here:

```
<link rel="localizations" href="langs.json" type=
  "application/l10n+json"/>
```

8. Define the `onload` function for the `body` tag to load the document initially with correct language values:

```
<body onload="onLoad();">
```

9. Create some HTML elements to try working with multiple languages. For this example, we will create two buttons, an alert box, and a heading tag. When the language is changed, all the string values will be changed too:

```
<h1 data-l10n-id="welcome">Welcome</h1>
<button data-l10n-id="french" onclick="changeToFrench()">
  French</button>
<button data-l10n-id="english" onclick="changeToEnglish()">
  English</button>
<button data-l10n-id="alert" onclick="showAlert()">Test
  Alert</button>
```

10. Create a function to be used to initialize the language settings. The `localize` method is used to load the application with the provided language. Initially, we load the page with the English language using the `index` method:

```
function onLoad() {
  html10n.index();
  html10n.localize('en');
}
```

11. Create two functions to load the English and French languages when users click on the button:

```
function changeToFrench() {
  html10n.localize('fr');
}

function changeToEnglish() {
  html10n.localize('en');
}
```

12. Define the function to show an alert window with the translated string when the **Test Alert** button is clicked:

```
function showAlert() {
  var message = html10n.get('alert');
  alert(message);
}
```

13. Apart from these, you can define your `deviceready` event function for other PhoneGap/Cordova-related activities. For this example, it's left empty:

```
document.addEventListener("deviceready", onDeviceReady, false);

function onDeviceReady() {
  // Other Stuffs
}
```

14. Open the command-line tool, go to the `Globalization` folder, and build and run the app on a real device or an emulator:

```
$ cordova build
$ cordova run
```

The complete source code of the example is provided here for your reference:

```
<!DOCTYPE html>
<html>
<head>
  <script type="text/javascript" src="js/l10n.js"></script>
  <link rel="localizations" href="langs.json" type="application/
    l10n+json"/>
</head>
<body onload="onLoad();">
  <h1 data-l10n-id="welcome">Welcome</h1>
  <button data-l10n-id="french" onclick="changeToFrench()">
    French</button>
  <button data-l10n-id="english" onclick="changeToEnglish()">
    English</button>
  <button data-l10n-id="alert" onclick="showAlert()">Test Alert
    </button>

  <script type="text/javascript">
    document.addEventListener("deviceready", onDeviceReady, false);

    function onDeviceReady() {
      // Other Stuffs
    }

    function onLoad() {
      html10n.index();
      html10n.localize('en');
    }

    function changeToFrench() {
```

```
      html10n.localize('fr');
    }

    function changeToEnglish() {
      html10n.localize('en');
    }

    function showAlert() {
      var message = html10n.get('alert');
      alert(message);
    }

  </script>
</body>
</html>
```

What just happened?

You developed an app that is able to render different text messages based on the language required by the user. When the user clicks on the **French/English** button, all other texts in the application will change automatically.

Adding multitouch gesture support

For any hybrid mobile apps, touch gestures is an important feature that makes the app great in the hands of the users.

The following is the list of JavaScript libraries that can enable multitouch gesture handling in your apps. Each library has its own merits and limitations. Some have dependencies with other libraries and some do not. You have to be careful when choosing the libraries as it might introduce new dependencies to your application:

Library name	Dependency	URL
ZeptoJS	No	`http://zeptojs.com/`
EventJS	No	`https://github.com/mudcube/Event.js`
QuoJS	No	`http://quojs.tapquo.com/`
Hammer	No	`http://hammerjs.github.io/`
ThumbsJS	No	`http://mwbrooks.github.io/thumbs.js/`
jGestures	jQuery	`http://jgestures.codeplex.com/`
DoubleTab	jQuery	`https://github.com/technoweenie/jquery.doubletap`

Library name	Dependency	URL
Touchable	jQuery	`https://github.com/dotmaster/Touchable-jQuery-Plugin`
TouchyJS	jQuery	`https://github.com/HotStudio/touchy`

Although there are a few more libraries, Hammer is widely trusted for gestures support in mobile applications. Hammer is an open source library that can recognize gestures made by touch, mouse, and pointerEvents. It doesn't have any dependencies and the total minified size is less than 4 KB.

We will illustrate an example using Hammer to implement touch events in the application.

Time for action – implementing gesture support

Refer to the following steps to implement multitouch gestures in your app using the Hammer JavaScript library:

1. Open the command-line tool and create a new PhoneGap project called `hammer`:

   ```
   $ cordova create hammer
   ```

2. Using the command-line tool, add the platform you want to use for this test (Android, Blackberry, iOS, or Windows Phone 8):

   ```
   $ cordova platform add android
   ```

3. Download the Hammer-related files from `https://github.com/hammerjs/hammer.js` and save it in the `www/js` folder. You can find both `hammer.min.js` and `hammer.js` files in the download bundle from GitHub. You can just keep the `hammer.min.js` file and delete the rest.

4. Include the `hammer.min.js` file in your `index.html` file to start using Hammer:

   ```
   <script src="js/hammer.min.js"></script>
   ```

5. Add a `div` element named `touch` to the page body. This element will be attached to all the touch events we are going to create:

   ```
   <div id="touch">Try Me</div>
   ```

6. Now, let's create the event listeners for the "press" gesture and attach it to the `div` element we just created:

   ```
   <script type="text/javascript">
     var touchId = document.getElementById('touch');

     var hammer = new Hammer(touchId);
   ```

```
hammer.on("press", function(ev) {
  touchId.textContent = ev.type +" gesture detected.";
});
```

```
</script">
```

7. Open the command-line tool, go to the project folder, and build and run the app on a real device or an emulator:

```
$ cordova build
$ cordova run
```

When you try to apply a "press" action on the element, you will see that Hammer has detected your action and changed the text content of the element.

> Note that the Hammer library is very flexible for the developers. You can handle multiple gestures in a single event handler. In the following example, we have handled pan, swipe, drag, and touch gestures in a single function. However, overusing them can damage your application performance:
>
> ```
> <script type="text/javascript">
>   var touchId = document.getElementById(myDiv);
>
>   var hammer = new Hammer(touchId);
>
>   //list of events to be handled
>   hammer.on("pan swipe drag touch press", function(ev)
> {
>     touchId.textContent = ev.type +" gesture
> detected.";
>   });
> </script">
> ```

The pinch and rotate recognizers are disabled by default because they might interfere with the application's behavior. However, if you want to handle these two gestures in your application, you can enable them by calling them as follows:

```
hammertime.get('pinch').set({ enable: true });
hammertime.get('rotate').set({ enable: true });
```

You can also enable vertical or all directions for the pan and swipe recognizers as shown here:

```
hammertime.get('pan').set({ direction: Hammer.DIRECTION_ALL });
hammertime.get('swipe').set({ direction: Hammer.DIRECTION_VERTICAL
  });
```

For more details on all gesture recognizers and customization options, refer to `http://hammerjs.github.io/getting-started/`. Reading this documentation will help you to use Hammer with maximum efficiency.

Handling click delays

We have seen that a mobile application can support various touch gestures. With the introduction of new technologies, differences between web apps and native mobile apps are getting close to zero, but not actually zero. One such difference is how click events are handled in mobile apps.

When you click on a button, mobile browsers wait for 300 ms to actually trigger the click event for the button that you have clicked. The actual reason is that the mobile browser waits to see whether the user wants to perform a click or a double click. After the 300 ms delay, if there is no other tap, it's considered as a single click. However, if there are no event handlers for double clicks, the delay will be unnecessary. By overcoming these delays, you can make your app more responsible and less laggy.

We are going to see an approach to avoid this 300 ms delay using the library called **FastClick** that is available at `https://github.com/ftlabs/fastclick`. The steps are as follows:

1. Include `fastclick.js` in your JavaScript pack or add it to your HTML page as shown here:

```
<script type='application/javascript' src=
  '/path/to/fastclick.js'></script>
```

2. Define the `deviceready` event listener as you regularly do for other PhoneGap/Cordova functionalities:

```
function onBodyLoad(){

  document.addEventListener("deviceready", onDeviceReady,
    false);

}
```

3. Now, attach the FastClick functionality as shown here:

```
function onDeviceReady()
{
  FastClick.attach(document.body);
}
```

In some cases, you might need FastClick to ignore a few elements where double-click is possible. In those cases, you can add the `needsclick` class to the element as shown here:

```
<a class="needsclick">Ignored by FastClick</a>
```

 For some more advanced discussions related to this topic, refer to FastClick's GitHub page. If you are looking at an alternative approach suggested by Google, take a look at `https://developers. google.com/mobile/articles/fast_buttons`.

Summary

In this chapter, you learned how to create an app that supports the locale of the user using PhoneGap's Globalization API and to create a localized app that supports multiple user languages. More importantly, we saw how we can better handle multitouch gestures in the application.

In the next chapter, we will cover the topics that will help you in making the application ready for public release.

9
Getting Ready for Release

So far, you've created your app with PhoneGap, defined the building blocks of its interface, and learned to use various APIs provided by PhoneGap. In this chapter, you will consolidate the app architecture and learn how to prepare your app for your final release to the public. You can optimize your application using various methods to give your users a solid UX experience.

In this chapter, you will:

- Learn to compress your JavaScript and also learn why this is especially important for a mobile app
- Learn how to introduce JavaScript dependencies
- Learn more about template engines and how to compress template files
- Create fluid, multiple views of your app using PhoneGap
- Learn how to create hardware-accelerated transitions
- Discover how to use common code base for web and mobile platforms

Exploring JavaScript compression

In computer programming, we refer to the process of removing unnecessary characters from the source code files, and eventually concatenating them, as **file compression**. When dealing with web standards, we can compress any file type, including HTML, CSS, and JavaScript. The main goal of this process is to reduce the file size in order to speed up download time.

One of the benefits of compressing your source code when working with PhoneGap is performance improvement. When dealing with a mobile app, the files are compiled as a single file that eventually loads external data. However, when dealing with an app built using PhoneGap, the files, even if they are stored locally, have to be loaded in the browser (that is, the **WebView**). Smaller files will be executed faster, so the end user will get a better experience with a more responsive user interface.

You may think that what really matters on a mobile device is the memory consumption, and that compression will not cause a great reduction of memory usage because the original file and the minified one are interpreted into the same code. However, there are compression tools that can affect the runtime performance as well. The following sections discuss three of the most popular compression tools that may help improve the performance of your app.

Google Closure Compiler

Google Closure is a set of open source tools built in order to help developers speed up the development process of modern web applications. The project consists of a JavaScript optimizer, comprehensive JavaScript library, server-side and client-side template engine, and JavaScript style checker and style fixer. As a complete overview of Google Closure is beyond the scope of this book, we will focus only on the compiler.

One of the sentences that best describes the compiler comes from the online documentation:

> *"Instead of compiling from a source language to machine code, it compiles from JavaScript to better JavaScript."*

You can use the compiler in one of the following three ways:

- You can use it online at `http://closure-compiler.appspot.com/home`
- You can download a Java application from `http://closure-compiler.googlecode.com/files/compiler-latest.zip` and execute it through the command-line tool
- You can use the API provided by Google (see `https://developers.google.com/closure/compiler/docs/gettingstarted_api`)

When you open the online application, you can specify in the left pane the URLs of the scripts you want to compile, what kind of optimization you want to be applied to the output file, and if you want the output to be formatted for readability. On the right pane of the web application, you will get a report dealing with the original size and the optimized size of the file, the compiled code, a list of warnings, eventually some errors, and the POST data sent to the Closure Compiler APIs. The warnings provided refer to possible mistakes in the source code and optimization that can be performed. For a reference to possible warning messages, go to `https://developers.google.com/closure/compiler/docs/error-ref`.

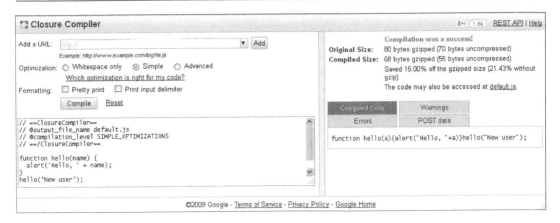

If you prefer working with the command-line tool, you can download the compiler application and execute it, specifying the compiling options and the input and output files:

```
$ java -jar compiler.jar --compilation_level ADVANCED_OPTIMIZATIONS --js hello.js
```

You get the same result when using the online tool; however, using the command line saves you an extra step: you don't have to upload the source code first.

When you use the advanced optimization, be aware that the renaming process will be more aggressive, the unused code will be removed, and the body of the function calls will be replaced with the body of the function itself (this process is known as **function inlining**).

Time for action – compressing files using the Closure Compiler

Follow the given steps to get a compressed and optimized file using the Google Closure Compiler:

1. Download and unzip the Closure Compiler application available at `http://dl.google.com/closure-compiler/compiler-latest.zip`.

2. Open the command-line tool, move to the unzipped folder, and create a folder named `sample`.

3. In the new folder, create three files: `index.html`, `test.js`, and `index.js`. You can use the following commands:

   ```
   $ echo '<!DOCTYPE html><html><head></head><body></body></html>' > index.html

   $ echo > index.js

   $ echo > test.js
   ```

4. Open the `test.js` file and define a self-executing function. Within the body of the function, declare two other functions and return one of them in order to be able to run this code from another JavaScript file (the purpose of the two functions is to mimic a real use case when some code is kept internal to a closure and some other is exposed through a returning object).

```
var test = (function(){

    var main = function(){

        alert('executing main');
        internal();
    };

    var internal = function(){

        alert('executing internal');

    };

    return {

        init: main

    }

}());
```

5. Open the `index.js` file and declare a variable in order to store the result of the self-executing function and make a call to the `init` function returned by the function itself:

```
var myTest = test.init();
```

6. Return to the command-line tool and run the compiler against the JavaScript files you just created:

```
$ java -jar closure-compiler/compiler.jar --compilation_level
ADVANCED_OPTIMIZATIONS --js samples/test.js samples/index.js --js_
output_file samples/app.js
```

7. Open the generated file and take a look at the source code; you will get the following JavaScript:

```
alert("executing main");alert("executing internal");
```

8. Insert the `script` tag in the HTML page referring to the new optimized JavaScript file and open it in a browser.

What just happened?

You discovered the potential of the ADVANCED_OPTIMIZATIONS compilation level of the Closure Compiler. As you can see, it's pretty aggressive. In fact, if you run the same command using the files you have created for your actual project, you will not be able to run the application as intended. In short, ensure to check whether the ADVANCED_OPTIMIZATIONS option breaks your code; if so, you should consider using a different level of compression.

Next, you will discover how to optimize and compress JavaScript modules using UglifyJS.

 In order to get an exhaustive guide to the Closure Compiler, refer to the online reference at https://developers.google.com/closure/compiler/docs/api-tutorial3 or just type $ java -jar compiler.jar --help in your command-line tool.

UglifyJS2

The **UglifyJS** project became very popular when jQuery started to use it. Being used by one of the *de facto* standard JavaScript libraries resulted in a lot of feedback to the author, which in turn helped him fix a number of bugs.

The new version of the project, named **UglifyJS2**, is slower than the previous one, but the overall compression results are much better and there are more advanced features such as multilevel source maps (basically, it's a way to map a combined/minified file back to an unbuilt state) like in the Google Closure Compiler.

UglifyJS2 is distributed as a Node.js module. In order to install it, you can proceed as with any other Node.js module. Open the command-line tool and use npm to install the uglify-js module:

```
$ sudo npm install uglify-js -g
```

At this point, compressing your JavaScript files just got a lot easier.

Time for action – using UglifyJS

Let's see how you can get a compressed version of the same files you worked on with the Google Closure Compiler:

1. Open your command-line tool and go to the sample folder created to test the Closure Compiler.

2. Type the following command in order to concatenate the JavaScript files and to run the UglifyJS2 compressor. For Windows, you can use the `copy` command to concatenate the files:

    ```
    C:\ copy /a *.js index.js

    $ cat test.js index.js

    $ uglifyjs --inline-script -o mytest.min.js
    ```

3. Open the generated file and take a look at the source code; you will get the following JavaScript:

    ```
    var test=function(){var main=function(){alert
        ("executing manin");internal()};var
        internal=function(){alert("executing internal")};
        return{init:main}}();var test=test.init();
    ```

4. Insert the `script` tag in the HTML page and open it in a browser.

What just happened?

You created a compressed version of two simple JavaScript files. As you can see, the output is rather different from the one created with the Closure Compiler. One of the main features of UglifyJS2 is that the generated output doesn't break the source code.

For a complete reference, you can check the project page on GitHub at `https://github.com/mishoo/UglifyJS2`.

 If you run UglifyJS2 in order to compress the files created in *Chapter 4, Working with Plugins*, you will be able to run the application as intended.

Optimization with RequireJS

RequireJS includes an optimization tool named **r.js** that combines related scripts together into build layers and minifies them via UglifyJS or the Closure Compiler. The tool can be used through Node.js or Java. When using the Closure Compiler, it's mandatory to run the tool using Java.

The optimizer is better than using a plain concatenation script because it runs RequireJS as part of the optimization, so it knows how to load the plugins and all the dependencies of the JavaScript modules needed in your application.

For an exhaustive guide to r.js, refer to the readme file available on GitHub at `https://github.com/jrburke/r.js`.

Time for action – optimizing JavaScript with RequireJS

Follow these steps to optimize the source code of your app using Node.js and RequireJS:

1. Install the `requirejs` module using npm from the command-line tool:

```
$ sudo npm install requirejs -g
```

2. Go to the root folder of the app you worked on in the previous chapters, create a file named `build.js`, and add to it the build process configuration info (that is, the JavaScript folder, the paths to the library used in the project, the name of the main file of the app, and the output folder and filename):

```
({
    baseUrl: 'js/',
    paths: {
        mustache: 'libs/mustache',
        alice: 'libs/alice.min',
        text: 'libs/require/plugins/text'
    },
    name: 'main',
    out: 'js/main-built.js'
})
```

3. Open the command-line tool again and execute the following command in order to build the app:

```
$ r.js -o build.js
```

4. Open the `index.html` file and change the entry point of your app in the `script` tag in the header:

```
<script data-main="js/main-built"
    src="js/libs/require/require.js"></script>
```

5. Open the `index.html` file in a browser.

What just happened?

You created a compressed version of the app's JavaScript files minified in a single file, specifying the command-line options using a build file. The result is that the code of the app is now optimized using UglifyJS2 (the engine that works behind the scenes) and it still works perfectly. In order to get a complete overview of the build options, refer to the sample build file available on GitHub at `https://github.com/jrburke/r.js/blob/master/build/example.build.js`.

If you prefer to use the Closure Compiler to compress and optimize the app's JavaScript files, you have to download the binaries of Rhino (an open source implementation of JavaScript written entirely in Java) available at `https://developer.mozilla.org/en-US/docs/Rhino/Download_Rhino`, download r.js from the RequireJS website at `http://requirejs.org/docs/download.html#rjs`, add the `optimize: 'closure'` option to the build file, and execute the following command:

```
$ java -classpath ~/rhino1_7R4/js.jar:~/compilers/
closure-compiler/compiler.jar org.mozilla.javascript.
tools.shell.Main r.js build.js
```

Here, `classpath` refers to the full path to Rhino and the Closure Compiler.

Comparing compression tools

We have covered three of the most popular compression tools. Each tool has its pros and cons. As always, the right tool for you is the one that best fits your needs. The following table summarizes the results, in bytes, you can get compressing a RequireJS file itself with the tools we just discussed:

File	Original size	Compressor	Size
RequireJS	82944	UglifyJS2	24576
		Google Closure	13312
		r.js	15360

As you can see, in this example, Google Closure yields the best result, but that is not always the case. If you run the same tests on the popular RaphaelJS library, you get the best result with Google Closure Compiler instead. The results vary depending on the source code writing style; for this reason, there is no single best tool to use. I prefer r.js because it can run the compressor engine as well as handle the plugins and module dependencies very well.

JavaScript task runners such as Gulp or Grunt can be used to create tasks to link, compress, and concatenate your resources automatically whenever there are some changes.

Other compression tools you may consider include KJScompress, Bananascript, JSMin, ShrinkSafe, and YUI Compressor.

Using template engine compression

When you work on larger HTML projects, it's advisable to use JavaScript templating engines and image compressions. When the application needs to be updated frequently with data, templating libraries will be of much use. I strongly believe that there is no such thing as *the* best JavaScript template engine. Each time you work on a project, you have to decide which is the right engine for the job at hand. For instance, **Underscore.js** templates are fast and lightweight and if you want them already loaded in your app, then it's a good option. When using jQuery, the natural choice seems to be **ICanHaz.js** because it returns each template as a jQuery object. When you need a more robust template engine, then **Google Closure Templates** could be a valid option. For a comparison of templating engines, visit `http://garann.github.io/template-chooser/`.

In most cases, **Mustache.js** completely fits the needs of an application because there is no logic in the templates and because the templates are language-agnostic, allowing you to reuse them between frontend and backend. There are several template engines based on **Mustache.js**, including **Handlebars.js**, **Hogan.js**, or **Pistachio**.

Handlebars.js is a superset of Mustache.js that adds some useful features such as block expressions, helpers, and more (refer to the online documentation at `http://handlebarsjs.com/` for a complete overview).

Hogan.js is a very powerful compiler for Mustache.js templates from Twitter. Hogan.js is also delivered with a command-line utility that compiles all the `*.mustache` templates stored in a folder; the utility is located in the `hogan.js-template/bin` folder. More information about Hogan.js is available on GitHub at `https://github.com/twitter/hogan.js`.

Pistachio is not just another JavaScript template engine based on Mustache.js. Its package contains a pure JavaScript compiler that compiles templates into self-contained JavaScript functions that can be used in every JavaScript environment.

In order to start using Pistachio's compiler, you can install it as a Node.js module:

```
$ sudo npm install pistachio -g
```

Once installed, you can compile a template by typing `pistachio` followed by the path to the file you want compile.

The interesting features of Pistachio's compiler are the capability to compile a template as an AMD module or CommonJS compatible module and the possibility to create the output as a jQuery object. A template compiled with Pistachio is still dynamic and can be compressed even more using the Google Closure Compiler. For a complete reference on Pistachio, go to `https://npmjs.org/package/pistachio`.

A compressed template speeds up your application rendering because you can cache it as a JavaScript function and avoid continuously loading and unloading it with an **AJAX** request (with some performance penalties involved) when the app is in use.

> If you want to include multiple templates in a file, you can simply store them in script tags, assign an ID to each tag, and then use the getElementByID() document object method and the innerHTML HTMLElement object property to render it:
>
> ```
> <script type="text/x-mustache" id="tid...">
>     /* mustache template */
> </script>
> ```

Time for action – compiling a template using Pistachio

Create a new template file and eventually compress it using Pistachio. Follow the given steps:

1. Open your command-line tool and move to the folders containing the template files.

2. Type the pistachio command and specify the name of the output file and the file to compile:

   ```
   $ pistachio --out=splash-tpl.js splash-tpl.html
   ```

3. Create a build file named, for instance, template-build.js, for the existing template to use when compressing the file with UglifyJS2, specifying the template name and the desired output filename:

   ```
   ({
       name: 'splash-tpl',
       out: 'splash-built.js'
   })
   ```

4. Run the r.js Node module from the command-line tool:

   ```
   $ r.js -o template-build.js
   ```

5. Open the file and check its syntax and size.

What just happened?

You created a compressed version of the template file that is stored in a variable. You can now request it in the modules of the app and avoid any unnecessary XMLHttpRequest.

This technique is most beneficial when working with pretty big and complex templates. Throughout this book, you will discover some advanced template caching techniques.

Creating fluid, multiple app views

One of the strengths of PhoneGap is that the app UI and logic are built upon web standards. A mobile app is made up of several views that allow the user to interact with its core features. As for a web app, when working with PhoneGap, you can think of a view as a web page or a fragment of a web page.

You can create multiple views in your app using different HTML pages or dynamically changing the markup of a single HTML page. The first approach is usually known as **multipage pattern**; the second one is known as **single-page pattern**.

Generally speaking, the multipage pattern is best suited to applications that mostly comprise static content or applications that rely mostly on the server for the business logic. When most of the content is static, you can package it using PhoneGap and deliver it as an app. When the business logic is defined on the server, you can think of the client as the presentation layer of your app and rely on a good mobile connection to make it available to users. In both cases, your client-side code should be pretty simple and easy to maintain.

The multipage approach has some disadvantages. For instance, when the user navigates from one page to the next, the browser has to reload and parse all the JavaScript associated with the new page. Also, because the JavaScript code is reloaded, all application state is lost if your app does not use other techniques such as local storage or the HTML5 history state object to maintain it.

The single-page pattern overcomes the disadvantages associated with the multipage approach. The PhoneGap and app JavaScript code is loaded just once, removing the need to pass application state from one page to the next. The disadvantage of this approach is an increased complexity of the JavaScript that contains most of the business logic and that it is required to update the UI when navigation occurs. Single-page applications are best written using the MVC design pattern and libraries such as AngularJS can be used.

The most important difference between the two patterns is that with the single-page pattern, the PhoneGap JavaScript bridge is loaded once. There's a noticeable pause when it's loaded due to the fact that the link between the JavaScript APIs and the native counterparts is created. When the app loads the PhoneGap JavaScript API once, the UI appears more responsive and the user experience is improved.

Using hardware-accelerated transitions

Much has been said about the use of **graphics processing unit (GPU)** hardware acceleration in smartphone and tablet web browsers. The general scheme is to offload tasks that would otherwise be calculated by the main CPU to the GPU in your computer's graphics adapter. (For a very detailed article to better understand hardware-accelerated transitions, go to `https://dev.sencha.com/blog/understanding-hardware-acceleration-on-mobile-browsers`.)

GPU can accelerate the following:

- The general layout compositing
- All the CSS transitions
- The CSS 3D transformations
- All the canvas drawing operations

You can create smooth animations with the new CSS transitions by pretty easily defining them in your style sheets or you can rely on external libraries.

CSS transitions are supported in the latest versions of Firefox, Safari, and Chrome. They're supported in IE 10 and above. If CSS animations aren't supported in a given browser, then the properties will be applied instantly, gracefully degrading. There are several techniques to handle a CSS transition. I will use **Alice.js**, which is an interesting JavaScript library that allows you to execute hardware-accelerated transitions in your app.

AliceJS

AliceJS (A Lightweight Independent CSS Engine) is a JavaScript library that leverages hardware-accelerated capabilities of browsers in order to generate visual effects. One of the strengths of the library is that it doesn't rely on other libraries and that it's self-contained in a single JavaScript file (for a complete reference and some interesting examples, refer to the official website at `http://blackberry.github.com/Alice/demos/index.html`.)

Each time you want to create a transition with AliceJS, you have to set up a configuration object. This object varies depending on the effect or plugin you are using. However, some configuration properties are shared between all the effects and plugins, including the following:

- `elems`: This is the target element(s) or node
- `rotate`: This is the rotation angle in degrees
- `perspectiveOrigin`: This is the anchor point, which can be `top-left`, `top-center`, `top-right`, `center`, and so on, or the explicit coordinates in percentage of the entire size of `div`, for example, `{x: 200, y: 200}`

- ◆ `duration`: This is the duration of the effect
- ◆ `timing`: This is the easing function as per standard CSS specs
- ◆ `delay`: This determines how long before the animation starts
- ◆ `iteration`: This is the number of iterations
- ◆ `direction`: This specifies whether the animation should be played in reverse mode
- ◆ `playstate`: This is either `running` or `paused`

In this way, it's possible to easily configure a CSS-based animation without any additional required know-how. There are three plugins for AliceJS and they include a few animation types. The following is the simple code from the Alice documentation to create a wobble effect by using the Cheshire plugin. So, we need to include the core and the plugin file:

```html
<div id="DIV1">HERE IS ONE DIV</div>
<img id="IMG1" src="/myimg.gif">
<script src="/alice/alice.core.js"></script>
<script src="/alice/alice.plugins.cheshire.js"></script>

<script>
alicejs.wobble({
    elems: ["DIV1", "IMG1"],
    rotate: 5,
    perspectiveOrigin: "center",
    duration: "200ms",
    timing: "linear",
    delay: "0ms",
    iteration: "infinite",
    direction: "alternate",
    playstate: "running"
});
</script>
```

As you can see, the code is pretty simple; for a complete overview, please refer to the online documentation of AliceJS.

Porting web applications

We know that PhoneGap/Cordova allows you to have a common code base for all mobile platforms. PhoneGap helps to package your HTML, CSS, and JavaScript code so that it can be installed in a mobile device and can be used as an app in different types of platforms such as Android, iOS, Firefox, and so on. It's not a surprise now. However, did you know that, with some planning, you can convert your existing web application to a hybrid mobile app?

If you are a web developer, you can even create a mobile app with your existing knowledge of web development and can sell in app marketplaces. You can save a lot of time and money by avoiding redevelopment.

PhoneGap/Cordova provides a lot of APIs to access device features such as the camera, accelerometer, and more. In this way, PhoneGap gives developers the ability to create a full-featured mobile app using web technologies. However, you can't use such device-related APIs in your web application. So, you have to design your code base so that it provides modularity.

The way a user interacts with an Android app is different from interacting with an iOS app and so on. So, there has to be careful planning on the design factors of the app. You might need tweaks on each platform to have a better user experience. You can use responsive design and media queries to target multiple screen sizes, devices, and display destinations (standard or high-density).

Providing a robust design for a common code base is beyond the scope of this book. However, there are lots of success stories of porting web applications to hybrid mobile applications.

Summary

In this chapter, you learned how to optimize the source code of your app and also how to compress the templates that you use; we also saw various code compression methods. With this, we have completed our learning and it's time to put them to work. In the next chapter, we will create an app to demonstrate all our knowledge of PhoneGap.

10
A Sample PhoneGap Project

Until now, we have seen how to create a PhoneGap project, use various APIs individually, and finally how to build the application. After learning these important things, we will need to package all our learning and create an actual app with all the APIs. Working on this demo app project will help you to understand the practical usage of the APIs and how to put them to use. I have tried to make the project as simple as possible, so that you can understand it without any difficulties.

In this chapter, you will:

- Create a new PhoneGap project
- Learn how to include Bootstrap and other libraries in the project
- Develop the demo app using all the APIs provided by PhoneGap
- Build the application and try it in a real device

What's in the app?

The demo app that we are going to create will showcase all the features of the PhoneGap/Cordova APIs. The app will list all sections in a sliding menu and the user can choose which API they are interested in. The demo app is available in the Google Play Store at `https://play.google.com/store/apps/details?id=com.iyaffle.phonegap.`

For the benefit of everyone, the complete project source is available in the GitHub repository. Readers can view or download the entire source from `https://github.com/iYaffle/PhoneGap-Demo-App`. Happy learning!

Libraries used

We are going to use the following libraries in our demo app. We will find out why we are using each of these libraries in our demo.

Twitter Bootstrap

Bootstrap is the most popular HTML, CSS, and JS framework for developing responsive projects on the web. Bootstrap will be our primary UI framework of the project.

It can be downloaded from `http://www.getbootstrap.com/`.

jQuery

jQuery is a JavaScript framework that has changed the life of many web developers. It has redefined the way JavaScript is coded. It provides an API to easily deal with DOM manipulation, event handling, animation, and AJAX.

It can be downloaded from `http://www.jquery.com/`.

mMenu

mMenu is the famous jQuery plugin that creates sliding submenus for websites and web apps. It has a dependency of jQuery and we will be using it to create our sliding menu.

It can be downloaded from `http://www.mmenu.frebsite.nl/`.

FastClick

FastClick is a tiny but useful library, which will help us to eliminate the 300 ms delay in touch devices. For more information on this, refer to the *Handling click delays* section of *Chapter 8, Advanced PhoneGap*.

It can be downloaded from `https://github.com/ftlabs/fastclick`.

This chapter will be a basic one and it's highly recommended for the readers to read the previous chapters to understand the APIs before proceeding. We have covered only the critical aspects of the project and the rest is left to the readers to read and interpret in order to encourage development of the project.

Creating the project

As the first step of our activity, we need to create a new PhoneGap project. We will be using PhoneGap CLI tools to create a project and install various plugins.

Now, let's create a new project named PhoneGap, using PhoneGap CLI:

```
C:\> phonegap create PhoneGap
```

After creating the project, as you know, a new directory with the project name will be created. Let's make that our current directory:

```
C:\> cd PhoneGap
```

Now, let's add Android as our target platform. If you are interested, you can add other platforms too, if you have the required SDKs installed:

```
C:\PhoneGap> phonegap platform add android
```

We should have the fastclick.js, jquery.mmenu.min.all, and jquery-2.1.3.min.js libraries downloaded in the js folder of the project's home www directory. Note that all CSS files of the jQuery and mMenu libraries should be placed in the css directory of the www directory. Now, we can kick off our project development.

Installing plugins

As our application is going to use almost all of the APIs, we will be installing them in our project. You can either install all of these plugins now or install them as and when required. The commands to install them are as follows:

- cordova plugin add cordova-plugin-dialogs
- cordova plugin add cordova-plugin-device
- cordova plugin add cordova-plugin-vibration
- cordova plugin add cordova-plugin-camera
- cordova plugin add cordova-plugin-network-information
- cordova plugin add cordova-plugin-contacts
- cordova plugin add cordova-plugin-splashscreen

- cordova plugin add cordova-plugin-device-motion
- cordova plugin add cordova-plugin-geolocation
- cordova plugin add cordova-plugin-media-capture
- cordova plugin add cordova-plugin-file
- cordova plugin add cordova-plugin-globalization
- cordova plugin add cordova-plugin-inappbrowser
- cordova plugin add cordova-plugin-media

Design of the homepage

For every app, the `index.html` page will be the homepage, and that's where our application will start too. To begin from scratch, clear out the body contents of the file. Inside the `<body>` tag of the `index.html` file, we will add the following code:

```html
<div id="page">
    <div class="header">
        <a href="#menu"></a>
        PhoneGap Demo Home
    </div>

    <div class="content">
        <div class="jumbotron">
            <h1>Welcome PhoneGap</h1>
            <img src="img/logo.png" />
            <p>
              <button id="openMenu" class="btn-lg btn-primary"
                onclick="">Start Here</button>
            </p>
        </div>
    </div>

</div>
```

To understand each of the sections in the preceding code, we will need to understand the Bootstrap components. In Bootstrap, we can have a header for the page that is identified by the `header` class. The actual contents of the page are placed under the `div` element with the `content` class. These are standard Bootstrap techniques and you can easily understand them if you read the Bootstrap documents.

Now, we'll add the CSS file references to the `<head>` section of the page, as follows:

```html
< link rel="stylesheet" type="text/css" href="css/demo.css">
< link rel="stylesheet" type="text/css" href="css/index.css">
```

Now, we will add all the required JavaScript files that we are going to use above the
`</body>` tag. Ensure that you are adding each file in the correct order, so that dependencies
are resolved:

```
<script type="text/javascript" src="cordova.js"></script>
<script type="text/javascript" src="js/jquery-2.1.3.min.js"></script>
<script type="text/javascript" src="js/
  jquery.mmenu.min.all.js"></script>
<script type="text/javascript" src="js/fastclick.js"></script>
<script type="text/javascript" src="js/main.js"></script>
```

You may have noticed that we have added a button with the `id` value as `openMenu`.
Now, we will add the event for it. We are trying to open the slide menu when the user clicks
on the button. The slide menu has become a famous approach recently, as it is used in the
Facebook mobile application:

```
<script type="text/javascript">
    $("#openMenu").click(function() {
        $("#menu").trigger("open.mm");
    });
</script>
```

With the provided CSS styling (refer to the `.css` files), you would see the app as shown in
the following screenshot:

Now, let's see the sliding menu. We have defined the menu content in a separate template file and we are going to include that in our page using AJAX. We will have the code in a separate JS file `main.js` so that we can include it in every page. The code snippet is provided here for your reference:

```
$(document).ready(function() {
    $.ajax({
        url: "menu.html",
        success: function(result) {
            $("#page").prepend(result);

            $("#menu").mmenu({
                "header": {
                    "title": "PhoneGap Demo Menu",
                    "add": true,
                    "update": true
                }
            });
        }
    });
});
```

The `menu.html` file will have a plain list with links to all the pages that we have created. Check that out for yourself here:

```
<nav id="menu">
    <ul>
        <li><a href="motion.html">Accelerometer</a></li>
        <li><a href="device.html">Device Info</a></li>
        <li><a href="camera.html">Camera</a></li>
        <li><a href="capture.html">Capture</a></li>
        <li><a href="connection.html">Connection</a></li>
        <li><a href="contacts.html">Contacts</a></li>
        <li><a href="file.html">Files</a></li>
        <li><a href="geolocation.html">GeoLocation</a></li>
        <li><a href="globalization.html">Globalization</a></li>
        <li><a href="browser.html">InApp Browser</a></li>
        <li><a href="notifications.html">Notifications</a></li>
        <li><a href="splash.html">Splash Screen</a></li>
        <li class="Spacer Label">This demo app is for learning
            only</li>
        <li><p>For bugs, issues & suggestions please create an issue in
            GitHub. Feel free to fork the GitHub Repo and contribute to
            make it better.</p></li>
    </ul>
</nav>
```

This code takes care of getting the content of menu.html and pushes that to the HTML document under the div element identified by the id value as page. Then, we apply the sliding option on the menu item that we have included.

After doing this correctly, when you click on the **Start Here** button, you will see the sliding menu open in front of you:

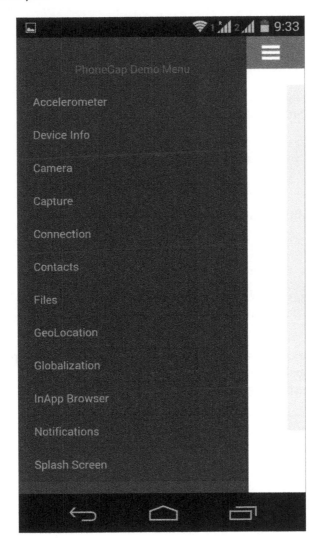

With this, we have made our basic framework of the app ready. Next, we will learn about each API and their usage. Going forward, only the main snippet will be provided. It will be helpful for readers to learn and try the rest themselves.

Using the Accelerometer API

We are now going to use the Accelerometer API. Using this API, we are going to get the acceleration coordinates and display them in the application. For the same, we have defined some div elements, as shown here:

```
<div class="content">
    <br/>Acceleration X :
    <div id="dataX">0</div>
    <br/>
    <br/>Acceleration Y :
    <div id="dataY">0</div>
    <br/>
    <br/>Acceleration Z :
    <div id="dataZ">0</div>
    <br/>
    <br/>TimeStamp :
    <div id="timeStamp">0</div>
    <br/>
    <br/>
```

Next, we have two buttons to start and stop the acceleration watch:

```
<button id="start" onclick="onDeviceReady();" style=
  "display:none;" class="btn-lg btn-success">Start
  Watching</button>
<br>
<button id="stop" onclick="stopWatch();" class="btn-lg btn-
  danger">Stop Watching</button>
</div>
```

Now, let's come to the core JavaScript for this. We are instructing the app to watch the acceleration continuously for one second, using the onDeviceReady() function and update the values in the corresponding div elements.

```
<script type="text/javascript">
    var watchID = null;

    document.addEventListener('deviceready', onDeviceReady, false);

    function onDeviceReady() {
        $('#stop').show();
        $('#start').hide();

        var options = {
            frequency: 1000
        }; // Update every 1 seconds

        watchID = navigator.accelerometer.watchAcceleration
          (onSuccess, onError, options);
```

```
        }

    function onSuccess(acceleration) {
        $('#dataX').html(acceleration.x);
        $('#dataY').html(acceleration.y);
        $('#dataZ').html(acceleration.z);
        $('#timeStamp').html(acceleration.timestamp);
    };

    function onError() {
        alert('onError!');
    };

    function stopWatch() {
        if (watchID) {
            navigator.accelerometer.clearWatch(watchID);
            watchID = null;

            $('#start').show();
            $('#stop').hide();
        }

    }
</script>
```

The output for this will be as follows:

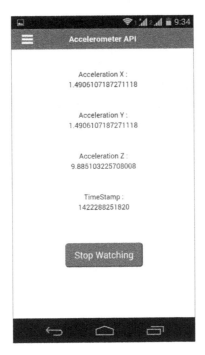

When we want to stop the watch, we trigger the `stopWatch()` function by clicking on the **Stop Watching** button. When we click on the **Start Watching** button, the watch will be started again, as shown here:

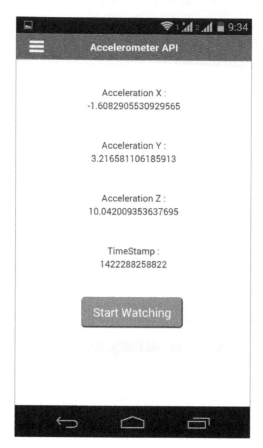

Using the Device API

With the Device API, we are going to get the information about our device. We will define five `<p>` tags to hold the data:

```
<p id="model"></p>
<p id="platform"></p>
<p id="version"></p>
<p id="uuid"></p>
<p id="cordova"></p>
```

We have the following script that will get the device information and put it in the DOM. You may have noticed that we are using the attribute ID value of the `<p>` element:

```
<script type="text/javascript">
    document.addEventListener('deviceready', onDeviceReady, false);

    function onDeviceReady() {

        $('#model').html(device.model);
        $('#cordova').html(device.cordova);
        $('#platform').html(device.platform);
        $('#uuid').html(device.uuid);
        $('#version').html(device.version);


    }
</script>
```

The output will be as shown here:

Using the Camera API

The Camera API can be used to capture an image from the device camera and also to select an image from the image gallery. We will see both of these uses with an example:

```
<div class="content">
    <ul class="nav nav-tabs">
        <li class="active"><a href="#capture" data-toggle="tab">
          Capture Photo</a>
        </li>
        <li><a href="#album" data-toggle="tab">From Album</a>
        </li>
    </ul>

    <div class="tab-content" id="tabs">
        <div id="capture" class="tab-pane active">
            <br/>
            <button onclick="capturePhoto();" class="btn btn-success"
              >Capture Camera Photo</button>
            <br/>
            <br/>
            <img style="display:none;" id="smallImage" src="" class=
              "img-responsive img-rounded" alt="Responsive image" />

        </div>

        <div id="album" class="tab-pane">
            <br/>
            <button onclick="getPhoto(Camera.PictureSourceType.
              SAVEDPHOTOALBUM);" class="btn btn-info">Select Image
              from Album</button>
            <br/>
            <br/>

            <img style="display:none;" id="largeImage" src="" class=
              "img-responsive img-rounded" alt="Responsive image" />
        </div>
    </div>
</div>
```

You will now be able to take photos, using your device camera:

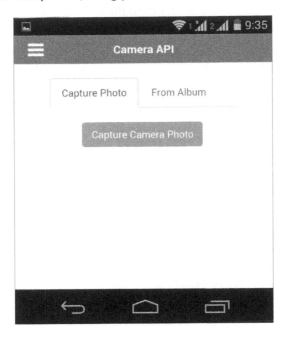

You will now also be able to select images from your device album:

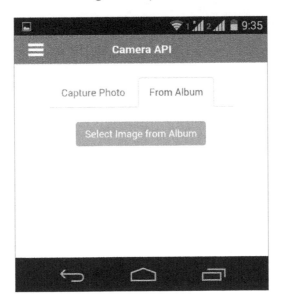

The following is the script used for this example and it's recommended that you read about the Camera API before proceeding with this example:

```javascript
<script type="text/javascript">

    function capturePhoto() {

        navigator.camera.getPicture(onPhotoDataSuccess, onFail, {
            quality: 50,
            allowEdit: true,
            destinationType: Camera.DestinationType.DATA_URL
        });
    }

    function onPhotoDataSuccess(imageData) {

        var smallImage = document.getElementById('smallImage');

        smallImage.style.display = 'block';
        smallImage.src = "data:image/jpeg;base64," + imageData;


    }

    function onPhotoURISuccess(imageURI) {

        var largeImage = document.getElementById('largeImage');

        largeImage.style.display = 'block';

        largeImage.src = "data:image/jpeg;base64," + imageURI;
    }

    function getPhoto(source) {
        navigator.camera.getPicture(onPhotoURISuccess, onFail, {
            quality: 50,
            destinationType: Camera.DestinationType.DATA_URL,
            sourceType: source
        });
```

```
        }

    function onFail(message) {
        alert(message);
    }
</script>
```

The following are the screenshots of the example in action:

Once you shoot the picture, you will be asked to select or reject the taken image:

Once you have accepted the image, it will be shown in the app:

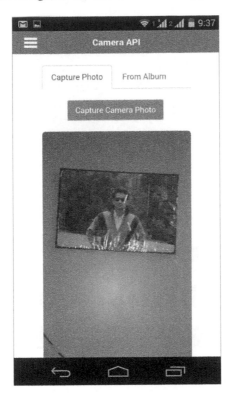

When you select the option to choose from the image gallery, the Gallery application will be shown for image selection:

Again, once you've selected an image from the gallery, it will be shown in the page:

Using the Capture API

With the help of the Capture API, we can capture audio, video, and camera images. We will see a simple code to perform all of these operations. The following code will add three buttons to the page and bind an event to each of those buttons:

```
<div class="content">
    <div class="btn-group-vertical" role="group" aria-label="...">
        <button onclick="captureAudio();" class="btn-lg btn-
success">Capture Audio</button>
        <br>
        <button onclick="captureImage();" class="btn-lg btn-
warning">Capture Image</button>
        <br>
        <button onclick="captureVideo();" class="btn-lg btn-
danger">Capture Video</button>
        <br>
    </div>

    <div id="details" style="display:none">
        <b>File Path : </b>
        <div id="fullPath"></div>
        <br/>
        <b>File Name : </b>
        <div id="name"></div>
        <br/>
        <b>Type : </b>
        <div id="type"></div>
        <br/>
        <b>Last Modified Timestamp : </b>
        <div id="lastModifiedDate"></div>
        <br/>
        <b>File Size (bytes) : </b>
        <div id="size"></div>
    </div>
</div>
```

The following is the JavaScript code snippet; each function is easy to understand:

```
<script type="text/javascript">
    function captureSuccess(mediaFiles) {
        var i, len;
```

```
        for (i = 0, len = mediaFiles.length; i < len; i += 1) {
            uploadFile(mediaFiles[i]);
        }
    }


     // Called if something bad happens.
    function captureError(error) {
        var msg = 'An error occurred during capture: ' + error.code;
        navigator.notification.alert(msg, null, 'Uh oh!');
    }


    // A button will call this function
    function captureAudio() {
        $('#details').hide();

        // Launch device audio recording application,
        // allowing user to capture up to 1 audio clips
        navigator.device.capture.captureAudio(captureSuccess,
          captureError, {
            limit: 1,
            duration: 10
        });
    }


    // A button will call this function
    function captureImage() {
        $('#details').hide();

        // Launch device camera application,
        // allowing user to capture up to 1 images
        navigator.device.capture.captureImage(captureSuccess,
          captureError, {
            limit: 1
        });
    }

    function captureVideo() {
        $('#details').hide();

        // Launch device video recording application,
        // allowing user to capture up to 1 video clip
```

```
    navigator.device.capture.captureVideo(captureSuccess,
      captureError, {
        limit: 1,
        duration: 10
    });
}

// Upload files to server
function uploadFile(mediaFile) {
    $('#fullPath').html(mediaFile.fullPath.replace
      (mediaFile.name, ""));
    $('#name').html(mediaFile.name);
    $('#type').html(mediaFile.type);
    $('#lastModifiedDate').html(mediaFile.lastModifiedDate);
    $('#size').html(mediaFile.size);
    $('#details').show();
    //Upload file using FileTransfer method not shown here
}
</script>
```

The output of this will be as follows:

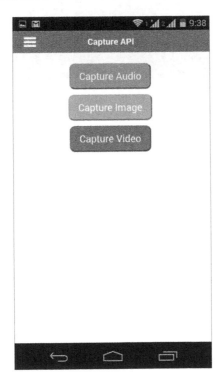

Try recording your voice using the app:

Using the Connection API

The Connection API is one of the simplest APIs to work with. We are going to find what kind of data connection the device has and then display it.

To hold the data, we define a new element, as shown here:

```
<p id="status" class="list-group-item-text">
```

In the JavaScript function, we get the connection type and validate it using the `checkConnection()` method. Then, we display a friendly message:

```
<script type="text/javascript">
  document.addEventListener('deviceready', onDeviceReady, false);

  function onDeviceReady() {
    checkConnection();
  }
```

```
    function checkConnection() {
      var networkState = navigator.connection.type;

      var states = {
      };
      states[Connection.UNKNOWN] = 'Unknown Connection';
      states[Connection.ETHERNET] = 'Ethernet Connection';
      states[Connection.WIFI] = 'WiFi Connection';
      states[Connection.CELL_2G] = 'Cell 2G Connection';
      states[Connection.CELL_3G] = 'Cell 3G Connection';
      states[Connection.CELL_4G] = 'Cell 4G Connection';
      states[Connection.CELL] = 'Cell Generic Connection';
      states[Connection.NONE] = 'No Network Connection';

      $('#status').html(states[networkState]);
    }
  </script>
```

The output of this will be as follows:

Using the Contacts API

Now, let's see some advanced concepts of the Contacts API. We are going to do the following three things:

1. Fetch ten phone numbers from a device; we have limited it to ten for simplicity.

2. Search for a contact and display their phone number, along with the contact name.

3. Add a new contact using the app.

The following is the HTML code; it looks big as we have used Bootstrap styles to create tab styles:

```html
<div id="page">
    <div class="header">
        <a href="#menu"></a>
        Contacts API
    </div>
    <div class="content">

        <ul class="nav nav-tabs">
            <li class="active"><a href="#fetch" data-
                toggle="tab">Fetch</a>
            </li>
            <li><a href="#add" data-toggle="tab">Add</a>
            </li>
        </ul>

        <div class="tab-content" id="tabs">

            <div id="fetch" class="tab-pane active">
                <br/>
                <button onclick="fetchContacts('');" class="btn btn-
                    info">Fetch 10 Contacts</button>
                <button id="searchName" class="btn btn-info">Search
                    Name</button>
                <br/>
                <br/>
                <div id="status"></div>

                <div id="panel" style="display:none">
                    <div class="list-group">
```

```html
<a href="#" class="list-group-item active">
    <h4 class="list-group-item-heading">Total
      Contacts</h4>
</a>
<a href="#" class="list-group-item">
    <p id="count" class="list-group-item-
      text"></p>
</a>
</div>

<table class="table table-striped">
    <thead>
        <tr>
            <th>#</th>
            <th>Name</th>
            <th>Phone Number</th>
        </tr>
    </thead>
    <tbody id="contacts">
    </tbody>
</table>

</div>
</div>
<div id="add" class="tab-pane">
    <form id="saveForm">
        <div class="form-group">
            <label for="firstName">First Name</label>
            <input class="form-control" type="text" id=
              "firstName" placeholder="Enter First Name"
              />
        </div>
        <div class="form-group">
            <label for="lastName">Last Name</label>
            <input class="form-control" type="text" id=
              "lastName" placeholder="Enter Last Name" />
        </div>
        <div class="form-group">
            <label for="email">Phone Number</label>
            <input class="form-control" type="tel" id=
              "number" placeholder="Enter Number" />
        </div>
```

```html
            <div class="form-group">
                <label for="email">Email Address</label>
                <input class="form-control" type="email" id=
                    "email" placeholder="Enter Email" />
            </div>
            <div class="form-group">
                <label for="note">Note</label>
                <textarea class="form-control" id="note"
                    placeholder="Enter Notes"></textarea>
            </div>
            <div class="form-group">
                <input class="btn btn-danger" type="button"
                    name="save" id="saveBtn" value="Save
                    Contact" />
            </div>

        </form>
    </div>

</div>
</div>
</div>
```

Coming to the JavaScript section, the following is the code for each operation. Reading the section about the Contacts API will help you to understand this. We have few jQuery-related statements too in the code:

```javascript
<script type="text/javascript">
    $("#searchName").click(function() {
        $('#status').html("");
        $('#panel').hide();

        navigator.notification.prompt(
            'Please enter search text',
            onPrompt,
            'Contact Search', ['Ok', 'Exit'],
            ''
        );
    });

    $("#saveBtn").click(function() {
        var firstName = document.getElementById('firstName').value;
        var lastName = document.getElementById('lastName').value;
        var fullName = firstName + ' ' + lastName;
```

```
    var number = document.getElementById('number').value;
    var note = document.getElementById('note').value;
    var emailAddress = document.getElementById('email').value;

    var theContact = navigator.contacts.create({
        "displayName": fullName
    });
    theContact.note = note;

    var emails = [];
    emails[0] = new ContactField('email', emailAddress, false);
    theContact.emails = emails;

    var phoneNumbers = [];
    phoneNumbers[0] = new ContactField('work', number, false);
    phoneNumbers[1] = new ContactField('mobile', number, true);
        // preferred number
    phoneNumbers[2] = new ContactField('home', number, false);
    theContact.phoneNumbers = phoneNumbers;

    theContact.save(onSaveSuccess, onSaveError);
});

function onSaveSuccess(contact) {
    navigator.notification.alert(
        "Contact Saved",
        null,
        'PhoneGap HandsOn Project',
        'OK'
    );

    document.getElementById("saveForm").reset();

}

function onSaveError(contactError) {
    navigator.notification.alert(
        "Contact Not Saved - Error Code : " + contactError.code,
        null,
        'PhoneGap HandsOn Project',
        'OK'
    );
}
```

```
function onPrompt(results) {
    if (results.buttonIndex == 1) {
        if (results.input1 == "") {
            navigator.notification.alert(
                "Empty Search Text",
                null,
                'PhoneGap HandsOn Project',
                'Try Again'
            );
        } else {
            fetchContacts(results.input1);
        }
    }
}

function fetchContacts(filter) {
    $('#panel').hide();
    $('#status').html("In Progress.... Please Wait!");

    var options = new ContactFindOptions();
    options.filter = filter;
    options.multiple = true;
    var fields = ["*"];
    navigator.contacts.find(fields, onSuccess, onError, options);

};

function onSuccess(contacts) {

    if (contacts.length == 0) {
        $('#panel').hide();
        $('#status').html("No Contacts Found");
        return;
    }

    var text = "";

    var totalCount = 0;

    for (var i = 0; i < contacts.length; i++) {
        if (totalCount > 9) {
            break;
        }

        if (contacts[i].phoneNumbers) {
            totalCount++;
            for (var j = 0; j < contacts[i].phoneNumbers.length;
j++) {
```

```
                    text = text + '<tr><td>' + totalCount + "</td>
                      <td>" + contacts[i].displayName + "</td><td>" +
                      contacts[i].phoneNumbers[j].value +
                      "</td></tr>";
                }
            }
        }

        $('#contacts').html(text);
        $('#count').html(contacts.length);
        $('#status').html("");
        $('#panel').show();
    }

    function onError(contactError) {
        alert(contactError);
    }
</script>
```

Ten contacts will be fetched and displayed when you click on the **Fetch 10 Contacts** button:

The total count of the contacts in the device and 10 contacts will be displayed, along with the phone number:

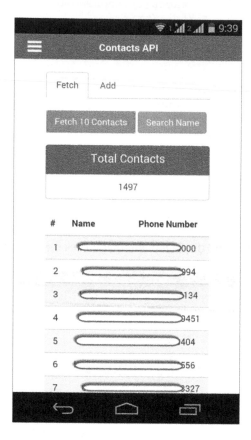

The contact names and numbers are hidden for the sake of privacy. You can also search for contacts, as shown here:

Once you enter the search text and click on the **OK** button, you will see the results for your search:

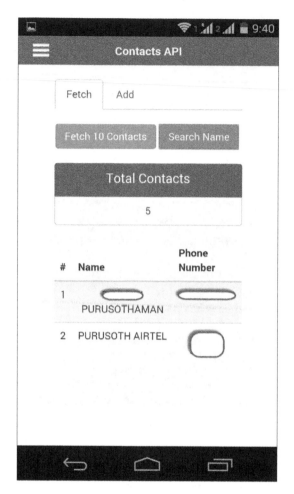

Using the Files API

Using the Files API, we can handle files and directories in the real device. This API makes it easy for the developers to handle all file-related operations:

```
<div id="page">
    <div class="content">
        <div class="btn-group-vertical" role="group" aria-
            label="...">
```

```
            <button class="btn-lg btn-success" onclick=
                "readDirectory()">Get All Directories</button>
        </div>
    </div>

    <div id="contents"></div>
</div>
```

The following is the code to get all the directories in the device filesystem. You can extend the code to read all files, as well as read, edit, and delete a file:

```
<script type="text/javascript">
    function readDirectory() {
        window.requestFileSystem(LocalFileSystem.PERSISTENT, 0,
            doDirectoryListing, null);
    }

    function doDirectoryListing(fileSystem) {

        var dirReader = fileSystem.root.createReader();

        dirReader.readEntries(gotDir, onError);
    }

    function gotDir(entries) {
        var s = '<ul class="list-group">';
        for (var i = 0, len = entries.length; i < len; i++) {

            if (entries[i].isDirectory) {
                s += '<li class="list-group-item">' + entries[i].
                    fullPath + '</li>';
            }

        }

        s += "</ul>";
        $('#contents').html(s);
    }

    function onError(error) {
        alert(error.code);
    }
</script>
```

The output will be as shown here:

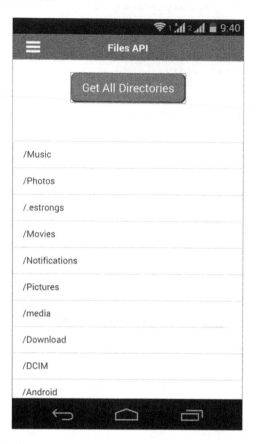

Using the Globalization API

The Globalization API helps you to customize content such as numbers, date, and currency based on your user's device locale, instead of showing them in a hardcoded format. With this API, you can truly create a real globalized application.

Let's create the menu for each of the options we are going to try:

```html
<div class="btn-group">
    <button type="button" class="btn btn-success">Globalization
      Menu</button>
    <button type="button" class="btn btn-danger dropdown-toggle"
      data-toggle="dropdown" aria-expanded="false">
        <span class="caret"></span>
        <span class="sr-only">Toggle Dropdown</span>
    </button>
    <ul class="dropdown-menu" role="menu">
        <li><a id="prefLang" href="#">Language</a>
        </li>
        <li><a id="locale" href="#">Locale</a>
        </li>
        <li><a id="pattern" href="#">Date Pattern</a>
        </li>
        <li><a id="numPattern" href="#">Number Pattern</a>
        </li>
        <li><a id="currPattern" href="#">Currency Pattern</a>
        </li>
        <li><a id="dateStr" href="#">Date to String</a>
        </li>
        <li><a id="strDate" href="#">String to Date</a>
        </li>
        <li><a id="monNames" href="#">Month Names</a>
        </li>
        <li><a id="dst" href="#">DST?</a>
        </li>
        <li><a id="firstWeekDay" href="#">Week First Day</a>
        </li>
    </ul>
</div>

<hr/>
<div id="data"></div>
</div>
```

With the preceding code, you will see the app as shown in the following screenshot; it has a drop-down menu for selecting the options to be used:

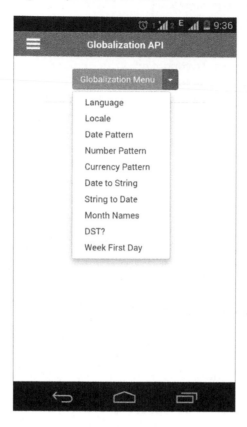

Now, the complete script is provided here; we have assigned each function to the click event of each link:

```javascript
<script type="text/javascript">
    $("#prefLang").click(function() {
        navigator.globalization.getPreferredLanguage(setLanguage,
            onError);
    });

    $("#locale").click(function() {
        navigator.globalization.getLocaleName(setLocale, onError);
    });
```

```
$("#dateStr").click(function() {
    navigator.globalization.dateToString(new Date(), setDate,
      onError, {
        formatLength: 'full',
        selector: 'date and time'
    });
});

$("#strDate").click(function() {
    navigator.globalization.stringToDate('12/31/2015',
      setStringDate, onError, {
        selector: 'date'
    });
});

$("#pattern").click(function() {
    navigator.globalization.getDatePattern(setPattern, onError, {
        formatLength: 'short',
        selector: 'date and time'
    });
});

$("#monNames").click(function() {
    navigator.globalization.getDateNames(setDateNames, onError, {
        type: 'wide',
        item: 'months'
    });
});

$("#dst").click(function() {
    navigator.globalization.isDayLightSavingsTime(new Date(),
      setDST, onError);
});

$("#firstWeekDay").click(function() {
    navigator.globalization.getFirstDayOfWeek(setFDW, onError);
});

$("#numPattern").click(function() {
    navigator.globalization.getNumberPattern(setNumPattern,
      onError, {
```

```
                type: 'decimal'
        });
});

$("#currPattern").click(function() {
    navigator.globalization.getCurrencyPattern('USD',
      setCurrencyPattern, onError);
});

function setCurrencyPattern(pattern) {
    $('#data').html('Currency Pattern: ' + pattern.pattern +
      '<br/>' +
        'code: ' + pattern.code + '<br/>' +
        'fraction: ' + pattern.fraction + '<br/>' +
        'rounding: ' + pattern.rounding + '<br/>' +
        'decimal: ' + pattern.decimal + '<br/>' +
        'grouping: ' + pattern.grouping);
}

function setNumPattern(pattern) {
    $('#data').html('Number Pattern : <br>' + pattern.pattern +
      '<br/>' +
        'symbol: ' + pattern.symbol + '<br/>' +
        'fraction: ' + pattern.fraction + '<br/>' +
        'rounding: ' + pattern.rounding + '<br/>' +
        'positive: ' + pattern.positive + '<br/>' +
        'negative: ' + pattern.negative + '<br/>' +
        'decimal: ' + pattern.decimal + '<br/>' +
        'grouping: ' + pattern.grouping);
}

function setFDW(day) {
    $('#data').html('Fist Day of Week : ' + day.value);
}

function setDST(date) {
    $('#data').html('Day Light Savings : ' + date.dst);
}
```

```
function setDateNames(names) {
    var str = '';

    for (var i = 0; i < names.value.length; i++) {
        str += names.value[i] + '<br/>';
    }

    $('#data').html('Month Names : <br/>' + str);
}

function setPattern(date) {
    $('#data').html('Date Pattern : ' + date.pattern + ' ' +
      date.timezone);
}

function setDate(date) {
    $('#data').html('Formatted Date : ' + date.value);
}

function setStringDate(date) {
    $('#data').html('Date : ' + (date.month + 1) + '/' + date.day
      + '/' + date.year);
}

function setLocale(locale) {
    $('#data').html('Locale Name : ' + locale.value);
}

function setLanguage(lang) {
    $('#data').html('Preferred Language : ' + lang.value);
}

function onError(error) {
    alert('code: ' + error.code + '\n' +
        'message: ' + error.message + '\n');

}</script>
```

When you click on the **Number Pattern** option, you can see the number pattern on the device that is decided based on the phone locale. Try out other menu options as well.

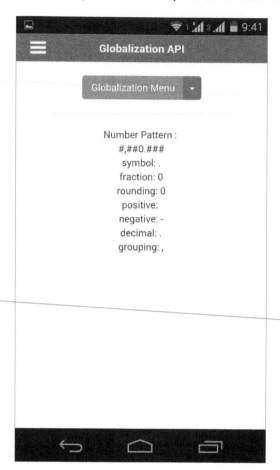

Using the InApp Browser API

InApp Browser is a web browser that can be controlled by the app. Your app can open the website in a browser and handle it as required.

Again, we will have a button to launch InApp Browser. We have created a JavaScript function named `launchIAB` to get the URL and open it:

```
<button onclick="launchIAB('http://www.incredibleindia.org');"
    class="btn-lg btn-primary">Launch Browser</button>
```

The output will be as shown here:

Now, we will see the JavaScript involved here. We have handled the load, start, and stop events of the InApp Browser:

```
<script type="text/javascript">            var iab = null;

        function loadStart(event) {
            // Event object has event.type & event.url properties
            alert('Loading started');
        }

        function loadStop(event) {
            alert('Loading stopped');
        }

        function loadError(event) {
            alert(event.type + ' - ' + event.message);
```

```
}

function onClose(event) {
    alert('Browser Closed');
    iab.removeEventListener('loadstart', loadStart);
    iab.removeEventListener('loadstop', loadStop);
    iab.removeEventListener('loaderror', loadError);
    iab.removeEventListener('exit', onClose);
}

function launchIAB(url) {
    iab = window.open(url, '_blank ', 'location = yes ');
    iab.addEventListener('loadstart', loadStart);
    iab.addEventListener('loadstop', loadStop);
    iab.addEventListener('loaderror', loadError);
    iab.addEventListener('exit', onClose);
}</script>
```

The loading start screen will be as follows:

Using the Notification API

With the Notification API, we can make the phone beep, vibrate, show alerts, and input and confirm dialog windows. So for each of these five operations, we will have five buttons that each have a trigger event. We have styled the buttons using Bootstrap:

```
<div class="content">
    <br/>
    <div class="btn-group-vertical" role="group" aria-label="...">
        <button onclick="beepNow();" class="btn-lg btn-primary">Beep
          3 Times</button>
        <button onclick="vibrateNow();" class="btn-lg btn-
          info">Vibrate 1 Sec</button>
        <button onclick="alertNow();" class="btn-lg btn-success">
          Alert Notify</button>
        <button onclick="confirmNow();" class="btn-lg btn-warning">
          Confirm Notify</button>
        <button onclick="promptNow();" class="btn-lg btn-danger">
          Prompt Notify</button>
    </div>
</div>
```

The output will be as follows:

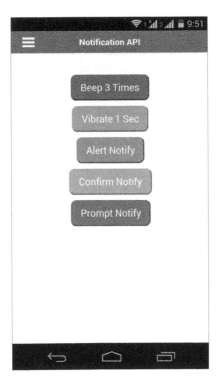

The following code is very much self-explanatory. Don't forget to take note of the syntax of the alert, confirm, and prompt dialog boxes:

```
function beepNow() {
    navigator.notification.beep(3);
}

function vibrateNow() {
    navigator.notification.vibrate(1000);
}
```

The preceding two functions will produce the default beep sound on your device three times and vibrate for one second, respectively:

```
function alertNow() {
    navigator.notification.alert(
        'You got an alert now', // message
        null, // callback
        'Notifications API', // title
        'Done' // buttonName
    );

}

function confirmNow() {
    navigator.notification.confirm(
        'You like this app?', // message
        onConfirm, // callback to invoke with index of button pressed
        'App Feedback', // title
        ['Yes', 'No'] // buttonLabels
    );

}

function onConfirm(buttonIndex) {
    alert('Button Selected : ' + buttonIndex);
}

function promptNow() {
    navigator.notification.prompt(
        'Please enter your name', // message
        handleAction, // callback to invoke
        'Registration', // title
```

```
        ['Ok', 'Exit'], // buttonLabels
        'Super Star Rajini' // defaultText
    );

    function handleAction(results) {
        alert("You selected button " + results.buttonIndex + " with
            input '" + results.input1 + "'");
    }

}
```

This is how the alert window is shown:

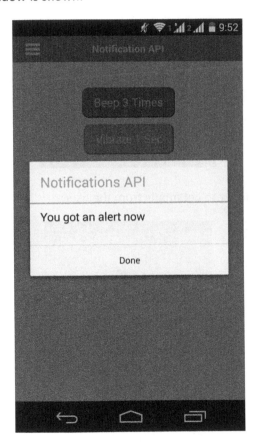

The confirmation box is shown in the following screenshot:

You can use the prompt dialog to get inputs from the user:

Using the Splash Screen API

Splash screens are the ones that you see when an application start. Although not all applications have it, It's available in some famous apps such as Microsoft Office Mobile. When the applications start, a fullscreen image shows up and closes automatically after a few seconds. This can be used to hide the backend loading of the application.

We will have a button with a click event to show the splash screen:

```
<button onclick="showScreen();">Show Splash Screen</button>
```

Coming to the JavaScript, we use the `navigator.splashscreen.show()` method to show the splash screen, as shown here:

```
<script type="text/javascript">
    function showScreen() {
        navigator.splashscreen.show();
    }
</script>
```

The output will be as follows:

When the **Show Splash Screen** button is clicked, you will see the splash screen open and close after a few seconds:

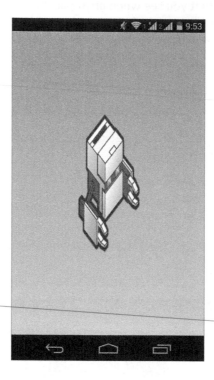

Note that there is also a function of hide(), and I am leaving that to you to try out.

Using the GeoLocation API

With the GeoLocation API, we are going to get the location coordinates and use Google Maps to plot them in a map:

```
<div id="page">
    <div class="header">
        <a href="#menu"></a>
        GeoLocation API
    </div>
    <div class="content">
        <div id="geolocation"></div>
        <br/>
        <div id="googleMap" style="width:75%;
          height:75%;">Loading...</div>
    </div>

</div>
```

The `div` element with `id` as `geolocation` will hold the geolocation values. The `div` element, `googleMap`, will have the Google Map:

```
<script type="text/javascript">
    document.addEventListener("deviceready", onDeviceReady, false);

var watchID = null;

function onDeviceReady() {
    // Throw an error if no update is received
    var options = {
        timeout: 50000
    };
    watchID = navigator.geolocation.watchPosition(onSuccess,
      onError, options);
}

function onSuccess(position) {
    var element = document.getElementById('geolocation');
    element.innerHTML = 'Latitude: ' + position.coords.latitude +
      '<br />' +
        'Longitude: ' + position.coords.longitude + '<br />' +
        'Altitude: ' + position.coords.altitude + '<br />' +
        'Accuracy: ' + position.coords.accuracy + '<br />' +
        'Altitude Accuracy: ' + position.coords.altitudeAccuracy
          + '<br />' +
        'Heading: ' + position.coords.heading + '<br />' +
        'Speed: ' + position.coords.speed + '<br />' +
        'Timestamp: ' + position.timestamp + '<br />';

    var myLatlng = new google.maps.LatLng
      (position.coords.latitude, position.coords.longitude);
    var mapOptions = {
        zoom: 4,
        center: myLatlng
    }
    var map = new google.maps.Map(document.getElementById
      ('googleMap'), mapOptions);

    var marker = new google.maps.Marker({
        position: myLatlng,
        map: map,
```

```
            title: 'Hello World!'
        });

    }

    function onError(error) {
        alert('code: ' + error.code + '\n' +
            'message: ' + error.message + '\n');
    }
</script>
```

The output will be as follows:

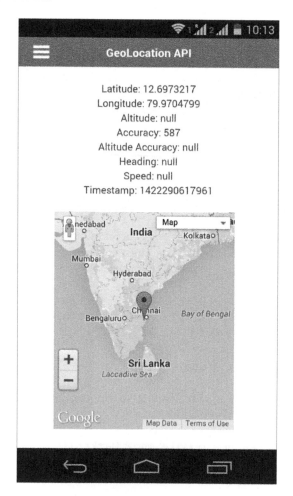

Building the app

As we have completed the development of the application, we can now build and try the app in a real device. You can either use a local build or build using the online PhoneGap services.

To use the local build using Cordova, use the following command:

```
C:\PhoneGap> phonegap build
```

After the build is complete, the app will be created for all the platforms you added when you created the project. You can see the Android app (.apk) inside the `platforms\android\ant-build\` directory and the iOS app (.ipa) inside `platforms/ios/build/device`, if you have added the iOS platform.

You can take the Android .apk file and directly install it in the device. However, for iOS, you need to perform provisioning. The details are covered in *Appendix B, Publishing Your App*. Congratulations on creating our full-fledged app using PhoneGap. Now, install the app in your real device and enjoy the feel of using your first full-fledged application.

Scope for improvements

The app that we saw is very basic and there is a lot of scope for improvements. The following are a few things that can be done to the app we just finished:

- Use a templating engine such as HandleBarJS
- Use the Ionic framework
- Use RequireJS to dynamically load the required libraries
- Handle hardware-accelerated, GPU-based animations
- Compress source files

Summary

We have learned how to create an app using PhoneGap and its API. This is just a start and there are many more challenges in creating a real-life app. We hope this tutorial will be a good foundation for your skills on hybrid app development. PhoneGap development is not limited to these APIs and there are several other useful plugins to be used. We wish you good luck for your PhoneGap development.

The JavaScript Quick Cheat Sheet

This is a mini cheat sheet for commonly used JavaScript methods and properties. For the complete list and documentation, please refer to the Mozilla Developer Network website available at `http://developer.mozilla.org/en/docs/JavaScript`.

The getElementById() method

The `getElementById()` method returns a reference to the element by its ID:

```
var pic =document.getElementById("profilePic");
```

The getElementsByTagName() method

The `getElementsByTagName()` method returns a collection of elements with the given tag name. The complete document is searched, including the root node:

```
var allImages =document.getElementsByTagName("img");
```

The getElementsByName() method

The `getElementsByName()` method returns a reference to the element by its name:

```
var names =document.getElementsByName("name");
```

The alert method

The `alert()` method displays an alert dialog with the optional specified content and an OK button:

```
alert("This is a sample alert");
```

The toString() method

The `toString()` method returns a string representing the source code of the function:

```
var countries = ["U.S.A", "U.K", "India", "France"];
alert(countries.toString());
```

The parseInt() method

The `parseInt()` method accepts a string and returns the numerical value. It can be used to convert a string type to a numeric type. For float values, `parseFloat()` can be used:

```
var stringOne = "1";
var intOne = parseInt(stringOne);
```

The getDate() method

The `getDate()` method returns the day of the month for the specified date according to local time:

```
var day = new Date();
alert(day.getDate())
```

The onclick event

The `onclick` event is fired when a pointing device button (usually a mouse button) is pressed and released on a single element:

```
<button onclick="callFunction()">Click</button>

<script>
function callFunction() {
    alert("Button Clicked");
}
</script>
```

The ondblclick event

The `ondblclick` event is fired when a pointing device button (usually a mouse button) is clicked twice on a single element:

```
<button ondblclick="callFunction()">Click</button>
<script>
function callFunction() {
    alert("Button Double Clicked");
}
</script>
```

The window.location object

The `window.location` object returns a `Location` object with information about the current location of the document. It can be used without the `window` prefix too.

The `window.location.href` object returns the URL of the current page:

```
alert(window.location.href);
```

Selectors using jQuery

If you are using jQuery in your project, you must know how easy it is to use selectors with jQuery. It provides convenient methods to select elements instead of using multiple JavaScript functions:

- `$("p")`: This selects element by tag name
- `$("#myID")`: This selects element based on the `id` attribute
- `$(".myClass")`: This selects element based on the `class` attribute

For more details on advanced jQuery selectors, visit `http://www.w3schools.com/jquery/jquery_selectors.asp`.

B
Publishing Your App

One of the best features of PhoneGap is that it allows you to create a cross-platform app using the same code base. It means that you can reuse most of the code, but you still have to build the app for each target platform. You can do this by configuring the development environment for each platform you want to support or you can use online services such as PhoneGap Build services (http://build.phonegap.com) or Icenium (http://www.icenium.com/). Both are cloud-based services; the main difference is that the PhoneGap Build service supports all the platforms, whereas Icenium supports only the Android and iOS platforms but does come with a very nice online editor. Once the builds are ready, you have to follow a different workflow for each target platform.

 Also, if you are dealing with cross-platform development when using PhoneGap, it's always a good habit to use a testing device for each platform during the development phase and when preparing the build.

Publishing on Google Play

Google Play, formerly known as the **Android Market**, is the digital application distribution platform for Android apps. In order to publish an app on Google Play, you have to log in with your Google account and follow the steps outlined at https://play.google.com/apps/publish. When registering, you will be required to pay a one-time fee of $ 25 before adding the developer details (that is, name, telephone number, e-mail, and so on). Once you complete the registration process, you can add your apps to the developer console.

For each app, you can define the countries in which you want to distribute it, define the carriers you want to target, specify whether it's a free app (if you want to sell an app, you have to provide a valid Google Wallet merchant account), set up an alpha and beta group for testing and the staged rollouts, and so on. In order to get new users to download and install the app, it's very important to provide detailed information, icons, screenshots, and so on.

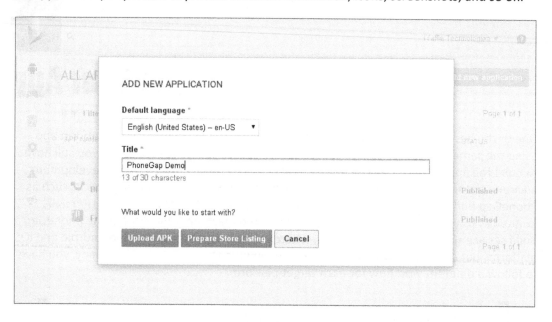

The Android online guide available at `https://support.google.com/googleplay/androiddeveloper/answer/1078870` is the place to start in order to get a better understanding of the required graphic assets.

In addition, your app has to be less than 50 MB in size and signed using the keystore tool as described at `http://developer.android.com/tools/publishing/app-signing.html`. For apps that require more than 50 MB, see the APK expansion details at `http://developer.android.com/google/play/expansion-files.html`.

 Once uploaded, your app will be available on the Google Play market within 60 minutes or less.

Publishing on Blackberry World

BlackBerry World (previously **BlackBerry App World**) is an application distribution service and an application by BlackBerry that allows users to browse, download, and update third-party applications. In order to publish an app on the BlackBerry World market, you need to have a BlackBerry developer account (you can create this for free at `https://developer.blackberry.com/`). You also need to apply to become a vendor providing your BlackBerry ID information (a PayPal account is required to complete the application), which you can do at `https://appworld.blackberry.com/isvportal/home.do`.

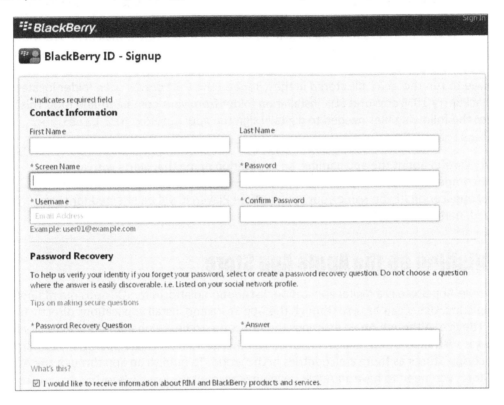

After you submit your application as a vendor, you will receive a confirmation e-mail asking you to provide official documentation to validate your company information or a copy (front and back) of an official government-issued identification card in case you applied as an individual to the vendor portal.

 The verification process can take up to two days, so you have to consider it carefully when you are planning a release for a specific date.

When your account is confirmed, you can add an app (that is, a product) providing the name, description, logo, screenshots, and any other required details about your application. For details on the requirements, refer to the online information available at the BlackBerry World app store at `https://developer.blackberry.com/devzone/blackberryworld/preparing_your_app_for_blackberry_world.html`.

The release of an app to the BlackBerry World also involves a signing process. This process assumes that you already have downloaded and installed the BlackBerry 10 WebWorks SDK available at `https://developer.blackberry.com/html5/downloads/`. Before you can get your BlackBerry 10 app signed, you have to complete the web form at `https://www.blackberry.com/SignedKeys`. When your application is accepted, you will receive two `.csj` registration files by e-mail. Each file arrives in a separate e-mail message with information about the purpose of the file attached (one is to generate a debug token and one to sign the app for the marketplace). In order to register with the RIM Signing Authority, you have to run the `.bar` file stored in the `\dependencies\tools\bin` folder located in the BlackBerry 10 WebWorks SDK installation folder from your command-line tool. This tool creates the following files needed to digitally sign the app: `author.p12`, `barsigner.csk`, and `barsigner.db`.

Be very careful about the app naming; an application name that starts with a brand/company/product implies an association and that it's an authorized or an official application. If you name your app YouTube Player, it will be rejected for sure (instead, name it Player for YouTube).

Publishing on the Apple App Store

The Apple App Store is a digital application distribution platform for iOS apps maintained by Apple Inc. Users can browse through the App Store and install applications directly to an iOS device. Although Apple envisions the App Store to be a global product, in reality its market is restricted by national boundaries. In other words, there are potentially as many distinct App Stores as there are countries in the world. To publish an app through the Apple App Store, you need to have an Apple Developer account (`http://developer.apple.com/programs/register`) and be a member of the iOS Developer Program (`http://developer.apple.com/programs/ios/`; the cost is $99 per year). The first step is to register an app ID with the developer portal and then you have to create the development and distribution certificates.

Then, you need to set up a distribution certificate. To do this, you will first need to generate a certificate request from your computer and then upload it to the developer portal. On a Mac, you should do this by opening the Keychain Access application available in **Utilities** and then go to **Keychain Access | Certificate Assistant | Request a Certificate from a Certificate Authority**. Enter your e-mail address and name and select **Request is Saved to disk** to save the `CertificateSigningRequest.certSigningRequest` file on your desktop. Go to the developer portal, upload the certificate request, and complete the steps required to generate the distribution certificate.

When the certificate is ready, you can create a new distribution provisioning profile by selecting the app you want to submit and the certificate to use. Download the file and in Xcode, select **Window | Organizer**, click on **Devices**, select **Provisioning Profiles**, and drag the provisioning profile with the `.mobileprovision` extension to the Organizer. Next, open the build settings pane and set the code-signing identity; in this way, the app is then code signed when you create an archive and you can complete the publication procedure using Xcode. When submitting the app, you will also be required to provide a description, several screenshots, icons, and other information. For details, refer to the online documentation at `https://developer.apple.com/library/ios/#documentation/IDEs/Conceptual/AppDistributionGuide/Introduction/Introduction.html`.

> The verification process varies depending on the number of submissions currently under review, but it typically takes more than two days. You can find the App Store's estimated review time at `http://reviewtimes.shinydevelopment.com/`.

Presenting a simple version of your app as first release will help to speed up the approval process a little bit. It's the initial app approval process that takes the most time; once approved, future updates are far easier to get done. So keep the advanced features for later releases of your app.

Visit `http://www.raywenderlich.com/8003/how-to-submit-your-app-to-apple-from-no-account-to-app-store-part-1` for a detailed tutorial on publishing an app to Apple App Store.

Publishing on the Windows Phone Store

The **Windows Phone Store** (previously **Windows Phone Marketplace**) is a digital distribution platform that allows users to browse and install applications that have been developed by third parties. The UI is presented in a very "Metro UI" way using a panoramic view where the user can browse categories and titles, see featured items, and get details with ratings, reviews, screenshots, and pricing information.

To submit and manage apps on Windows Phone Dev Center, you first have to register and become a member using a Microsoft account (formerly known as Windows Live ID). When registering, you will be asked to pay an annual Developer Center subscription fee of $99 plus any applicable tax. In exchange, you'll get to submit unlimited paid apps to Windows Phone Store (you can also submit up to 100 free apps). The publishing process is simple and straightforward: you have to provide the app details (name, description, screenshots, and so on) and then submit the XAP file packaged with Visual Studio. You must package and prepare your app before you can upload it to the store; the packaging process starts when you create a Windows Store project or item based on a template (refer to the online documentation at `http://msdn.microsoft.com/en-us/library/windows/apps/br230260.aspx` for a complete overview of the packaging process).

 The verification process is pretty fast, but you need a couple of days to complete the registration process if you are registering as a company.

In order to reduce the duration of the review, you can screen your app locally using the **Windows Application Certification Kit** (**WACK**) tool available in the Windows Phone SDK. It reduces the approval cycle by giving you a way to screen your app locally for issues before you even submit it to the Windows Store.

Summary

In this appendix, you learned how you can publish your app on different app stores and about common issues. It's pretty clear that the Apple store is the one that requires the most complex workflow, but it also attracts the most developers. You can easily manage publication on all the different markets by yourself or with the support offered by services such as the one by PhoneGap Build.

Related Plugin Resources

The following is a list of some related plugins that can be used with your PhoneGap:

- **Social Share**: This is available at `https://www.github.com/EddyVerbruggen/SocialSharing-PhoneGap-Plugin`
- **Facebook Connect**: This is available at `https://github.com/Wizcorp/phonegap-facebook-plugin`
- **Push Notifications**: This is available at `https://github.com/phonegap-build/PushPlugin`
- **Barcode Scanner**: This is available at `https://github.com/wildabeast/BarcodeScanner`
- **ActionSheet**: This is available at `https://github.com/EddyVerbruggen/cordova-plugin-actionsheet`
- **Bluetooth Serial**: This is available at `https://github.com/don/BluetoothSerial`
- **Calendar**: This is available at `https://github.com/EddyVerbruggen/Calendar-PhoneGap-Plugin`
- **Badge**: This is available at `https://github.com/katzer/cordova-plugin-badge`
- **Toast** (buttonless popup): This is available at `https://github.com/EddyVerbruggen/Toast-PhoneGap-Plugin`
- **Image Picker**: This is available at `https://github.com/wymsee/cordova-imagePicker`
- **Image Resizer**: This is available at `https://github.com/julianohaze/PhoneGap-Image-Resizer`

- ◆ **oAuth**: This is available at `https://github.com/oauth-io/oauth-phonegap`
- ◆ **Android InApp Billing**: This is available at `https://github.com/poiuytrez/AndroidInAppBilling`
- ◆ **Zip File Handling**: This is available at `https://github.com/Adobe-Marketing-Cloud/cordova-zip-plugin`
- ◆ **ngCordova plugins for the Ionic platform**: These are available at `http://www.ngcordova.com/`

Summary

We have provided some important plugins that may be useful in a real fully-fledged app. This is not a comprehensive list of plugins as it's not possible to provide the entire list in this appendix. You can search at `https://build.phonegap.com/plugins` or `http://www.plugreg.com` for more plugins and descriptions.

D
PhoneGap Tools

The PhoneGap Developer App

In earlier chapters, we have seen several ways to run/debug our PhoneGap project. The easiest way is to use the PhoneGap Developer App. It's a mobile application available for Windows, Android, and iOS platforms. Once you have installed the mobile application, you can easily test your project without actually building and installing the application on your physical device connected to the same wireless network as your desktop.

Once you have the project ready to test, you can use the `serve` command of the PhoneGap command-line tool to start a local server listening on an IP address.

```
Mark Administrator: C:\Windows\system32\cmd.exe - phonegap serve

C:\Users\purs\DeviceApi>phonegap serve
[phonegap] starting app server...
[phonegap] listening on 100.76.142.130:3000
[phonegap]
[phonegap] ctrl-c to stop the server
[phonegap]
```

Now, open the installed application in your device, enter the IP address listed on the command line, and click the **Connect** button. Now, your desktop computer and the mobile device will be wirelessly paired, and you can see your app on the device. Any changes made to the code will be instantly reflected on the device. The device APIs that do not work on browsers, will be working on your device even without installing the application.

More details and download links for all platforms can be found at `http://app.phonegap.com`.

The PhoneGap Desktop App

To make our life easier, we now have a desktop app and you are now free to use it, instead of the PhoneGap command-line interface. You can create a new PhoneGap project, import an existing one, and start the local server with a single click. It's still not a mature product and many features are getting added every month.

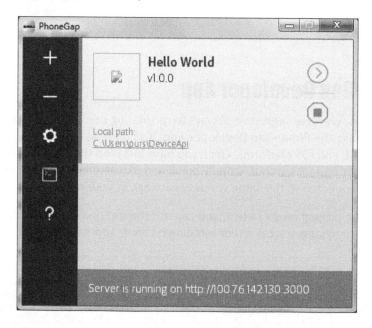

You can download the application for your Windows desktop or Mac OS at `https://github.com/phonegap/phonegap-app-desktop/releases`.

Summary

We have seen some recent PhoneGap-related tools available for developers to make hybrid mobile application development much easier. Both the Developer App and Desktop App will help you to debug and test your applications without many difficulties.

Index

R

related plugins resources
about 239, 240
ActionSheet 239
Android InApp Billing 240
Badge 239
Barcode Scanner 239
Bluetooth Serial 239
Calendar 239
Facebook Connect 239
Image Picker 239
Image Resizer 239
ngCordova plugins for Ionic platform 240
oAuth 240
Push Notifications 239
Social Share 239
Toast 239
Zip File Handling 240
RequireJS
using, for JavaScript optimization 169
using, for optimization 168
resume event 21
Rhino
URL 170
Ripple
reference 5
Ripple Emulator
URL 33
r.js
about 168
URL 168

S

selectors
using, with jQuery 231
Semantic Versioning
about 3
URL 3
SessionStorage API
URL 64
single-page pattern 173
Social Sharing
about 61
URL 61

Splash Screen API
using 223
SQLcipher 76
SQLite 70
StorageEvent, properties
key 65
newValue 65
oldValue 65
url 65
structure, PhoneGap application
config.xml file 18
hooks directory 18
merges directory 18
platforms directory 18
plugins directory 18
www directory 18
Symbian Web Runtime apps 5

T

target platform, SDKs
Android 7
BlackBerry 10 7
Firefox OS 7
iOS 7
Windows 8 Phone 7
template file
compiling, with Pistachio 172
toString() method 230
trilateration 139
Twitter Bootstrap
about 43, 178
URL 178
using 43

U

UglifyJS project
about 167
using 167
UglifyJS2 project
about 167
URL 168
Underscore.js templates 171
UQL (Unstructured Query Language) 70

Thank you for buying
PhoneGap Beginner's Guide
Third Edition

About Packt Publishing

Packt, pronounced 'packed', published its first book, *Mastering phpMyAdmin for Effective MySQL Management*, in April 2004, and subsequently continued to specialize in publishing highly focused books on specific technologies and solutions.

Our books and publications share the experiences of your fellow IT professionals in adapting and customizing today's systems, applications, and frameworks. Our solution-based books give you the knowledge and power to customize the software and technologies you're using to get the job done. Packt books are more specific and less general than the IT books you have seen in the past. Our unique business model allows us to bring you more focused information, giving you more of what you need to know, and less of what you don't.

Packt is a modern yet unique publishing company that focuses on producing quality, cutting-edge books for communities of developers, administrators, and newbies alike. For more information, please visit our website at www.packtpub.com.

About Packt Open Source

In 2010, Packt launched two new brands, Packt Open Source and Packt Enterprise, in order to continue its focus on specialization. This book is part of the Packt Open Source brand, home to books published on software built around open source licenses, and offering information to anybody from advanced developers to budding web designers. The Open Source brand also runs Packt's Open Source Royalty Scheme, by which Packt gives a royalty to each open source project about whose software a book is sold.

Writing for Packt

We welcome all inquiries from people who are interested in authoring. Book proposals should be sent to author@packtpub.com. If your book idea is still at an early stage and you would like to discuss it first before writing a formal book proposal, then please contact us; one of our commissioning editors will get in touch with you.

We're not just looking for published authors; if you have strong technical skills but no writing experience, our experienced editors can help you develop a writing career, or simply get some additional reward for your expertise.

PhoneGap for Enterprise

ISBN: 978-1-78355-475-1   Paperback: 192 pages

Master the art of building secure enterprise mobile applications using PhoneGap

1. Learn how to build secure mobile enterprise apps from scratch using PhoneGap.

2. Understand PhoneGap's framework, including common issues and their resolutions, and become the go-to person in your organization.

3. A concise guide that walks you through the best practices to build a secure enterprise application.

PhoneGap and AngularJS for Cross-platform Development

ISBN: 978-1-78398-892-1   Paperback: 122 pages

Build exciting cross-platform applications using PhoneGap and AngularJS

1. Create a simple web-based app using AngularJS.

2. Build PhoneGap apps for iOS and Android with AngularJS, HTML, and CSS.

3. Learn how to use PhoneGap's command-line interface to build mobile applications using easy-to-follow, step-by-step exercises.

Please check **www.PacktPub.com** for information on our titles

PUBLISHING

Beginning PhoneGap

ISBN: 978-1-78216-444-9   Duration: 01:49 hours

Write fully functional iOS and Android applications using cutting-edge PhoneGap techniques

1. Get the best of both worlds – traditional web technology and mobile app development – with PhoneGap.

2. Discover everything you need to know to build powerful cross-platform apps.

3. Develop, debug, and test your code easily through concise and simple examples.

PhoneGap 3.x Mobile Application Development HOTSHOT

ISBN: 978-1-78328-792-5   Paperback: 450 pages

Create useful and exciting real-world apps for iOS and Android devices with 12 fantastic projects

1. Use PhoneGap 3.x effectively to build real, functional mobile apps ranging from productivity apps to a simple arcade game.

2. Explore often-used design patterns in apps designed for mobile devices.

3. Fully practical, project-based approach to give you the confidence in developing your app independently.

Please check **www.PacktPub.com** for information on our titles

Lightning Source UK Ltd.
Milton Keynes UK
UKOW05f0650220516

274737UK00004B/188/P